MW01122304

SUPERPOWERING PEOPLE

Designing The Collaborative Digital Organization

By Oscar Berg

© Oscar Berg 2018
Publisher: Unicorn Titans, Sweden
Print: BoD – Books on Demand, Norderstedt, Germany
ISBN: 978-91-984700-2-4

ABOUT OSCAR BERG

Oscar Berg is an internationally recognized expert on social collaboration and the future of work. Besides being an appreciated keynote speaker, blogger, writer and author. Oscar is Business Designer and CEO at Unicorn Titans, a digital innovation agency based in sweden.

Twitter: @oscarberg
Webbsite: oscarberg.net
LinkedIn: se.linkedin.com/in/oscarberg

CONTENTS

DUMB BY CHOICE

by Simon Terry

Traditional hierarchical organizations are designed to make us dumb. These organizations work to deliver the predictable execution of a stable, proven business model. We have designed these organizations to exclude information from decision-making and isolate employees to focus on efficiency, predictability, and control. Without better ways of distributing and filtering information, we chose to create the many layers of management, channels of communication, and decision making processes. Each of these familiar elements of organizations limit the information we use and the way we work. The consequence was an improvement in efficiency, but limited adaptability to exceptions, challenges, and change. Our employees and our customers feel the costs of these limits. We have created organizations that treat people, whether customers or employees, as a cog in the machine of value-creation.

In the last century, with the opportunities presented by expanding global consumer markets, our dumbness, loss of human potential, and inflexibility were small prices to pay. There were real financial barriers to better use of information. The lost opportunities were overwhelmed by the ever-growing market opportunity. Most organizations used the same operating model and faced the same economics of information, so the threat of disruptive competition was muted.

As Oscar Berg highlights in this book, the competitive marketplace for organizations has now fundamentally changed. Information networks and digital capabilities have reduced the cost of creating and sharing information and expanded the access to information of businesses, consumers, and communities. Increasingly, organizations are dealing with knowledge work and complex situations.

The cost of a dumb process and the missed human potential is rising. Organizations can see competitors better leveraging the potential of their people to learn, to adapt, and to collaborate.

The challenge for managers and for employees in this new world, is how to change our ways of working and how we create, share and make use of information. We need our organizations to make us smarter. We need our organizations to help us to learn and to realize our collective potential. This book sets out to equip us all with some key tools to begin this redesign of the way we work.

GETTING SMARTER

Work has always involved people coming together to achieve more than one individual can do on their own. The most effective organizations enhance the knowledge, capabilities, and potential of their employees. Changing our ways of working to better use information and foster new forms of collaboration is a critical design element to the future of work. Rather than being passive participants in a process, employees can become a crucial element in the way our organization gathers, shares, and creates value from information.

In this book, you will find a number of key concepts and tools that will help your organization to realize the opportunities and the value offered by new models of social collaboration. Change is not easy. New capabilities will need to be learned and practiced. New mindsets will be required to foster effective communication. Ultimately, teams will need to mature their practice to work in increasingly valuable and visible ways. This book highlights these concepts, provides examples of the new approaches, and supports each of us to put them into practical use.

If we want to work in smarter ways and to see our organizations prosper, leadership is required. These changes to established ways of working won't happen on their own. We can't rely on technology to change established practice in our work communities. We will need change agents and leaders to take on the role of building new capabilities, advocating for new mindsets, and role modeling new practice. Adaptive leaders, collaborating in and beyond their organizations, will change established practice and help organizations experiment with the potential of new ways of working.

Take up the challenge of this book and experiment with new ways of collaborating in your organization. You have the opportunity to be well equipped to begin leading the change and making your organization smarter and more effective. Most of all, you will be contributing to making the future of work that much smarter and more human.

Simon Terry is a change agent, consultant, speaker and writer on learning, leadership and collaboration. Simon is also a board advisor to corporates, not-for-profits and startups. He works with organisations to help make the future of work more human and to enable organisations to better realise strategic value and the potential of people through new ways of working. Simon is owner and a charter member of Change Agents Worldwide and his writing can be found at simonterry.com

INTRODUCTION

"...we're starting to see that as business conditions change faster and faster with each year, and we cannot change our management hierarchical organization very fast relative to the changing business conditions. We can't have somebody working for a new boss every week. We also can't change our geographic organization very fast. As a matter of fact even slower than the management one. We can't be moving people around the country every week.

But we can change an electronic organization like that(snapping his fingers). And what's starting to happen is as we start to link these computers together with sophisticated networks and great user interfaces, we're starting to be able to create clusters of people working on a common task in you know literally in fifteen minutes worth of setup. And these fifteen people can work together extremely efficiently no matter where they are geographically. And no matter who they work for hierarchically.

And these organizations can live for as long as they're needed and then vanish. And we're finding we can reorganize our companies electronically very rapidly. And that's the only type of organization that can begin to keep pace with the changing business conditions."

Steve Jobs (("Steve Jobs interview", 1990)

When you think about it, isn't collaboration what an organization is about? Isn't an organization's reason for existence to bring people together to collaborate on a shared purpose? The better it is at collaborating, the greater the chances it will survive and thrive.

The 20th century was the era of the industrial corporation and mass production. Cost-effectiveness, time to market and economies of scale dominated the agenda of most corporations. In the name of efficiency, collaboration got encoded, automated and orchestrated in processes and systems. Soon collaboration was running in autopilot mode.

Today organizations operate in increasingly dynamic, competitive and unpredictable business environments. They need to be prepared for change and quickly adapt to changes in their environment. This means they cannot rely on the autopilot for collaboration any more. They need the spontaneity, flexibility and creativity that often characterizes collaboration in a small company or startup, but it must happen at a much greater scale and across geographical and organizational barriers. An organization's survival increasingly depends on its ability to mobilize and organize its people. information and knowledge using digital technology. To me, only one word is needed to describe this ability: collaboration.

A lot of organizations strive to become more agile and innovative. Doing so, they often rely on the same assumptions, thinking and methods that formed the basis of the traditional industrial corporation, and which worked against innovation and agility. They are also quick to jump to solutions without understanding the true nature of the problems they are trying to fix. They deploy new tools hoping these will 'automagically' fix problems without considering human behavior or culture.

The ambition of this book is to help you and your organization avoid these pitfalls. To do so, it questions existing assumptions, thinking and methods, and introduces new ones. It reveals the true nature of the problems that make organizations become conservative and rigid as they 'grow up', instead of remaining innovative and agile. It describes how digital tools can leverage wanted human behaviors and speed up a culture change, if these are designed with the people and the culture as the starting point. Along the way, you will learn why information is like water, why the hierarchical organization has passed its due date, and why you can find the clues for a solution to information overload in the ancient and long since destroyed Library of Alexandria.

CHAPTER 1

UNLEASHING
THE POWER OF SOCIAL
NETWORKS

"Throughout the primate world, social networks provide a fast conduit for innovation and information-sharing that help the group as a whole to adapt to its environment."

Alex Wright

Not that long ago it was possible for a business to make long-term detailed plans and execute the plans over a period of several years. They could, with fairly good accuracy, predict the demand for their products or services over years, and match supply accordingly. Consumers remained fairly stable in their attitudes and behaviors towards products and services. Everybody needed to buy a new fridge, car, or television set every decade or so, and since the needs didn't change that much over the years, nor did the products. Some new features and an updated design were all that was required.

A hierarchy of managers made sure that plans were followed and executed. The role of management was to execute the business model as efficiently as possible, focusing on cutting cost so they could increase their market share through competitive pricing, and increase profits and returns to shareholders. Management created and refined policies and procedures to make sure that operations ran like a well oiled machine, and all measures of success and incentive systems were geared towards efficient execution.

Today, the business environment is different due to global competition and rapidly changing attitudes and behaviors among consumers towards products and services. Organizations operate in an increasingly complex, unpredictable, and rapidly changing environment. Many of the challenges they have to deal with require the participation of lots of people, with different professions and skill sets, coming from different geographies, organizations and backgrounds. Whether the goal is to serve a customer, solve a problem, or develop a new product, the organization relies heavily on its ability to quickly mobilize and coordinate the right people, and to get the best and most out of the people it has available.

A lot of organizations perform poorly in these respects, especially those that are large or growing rapidly and have a physically dispersed workforce. They need to respond and adapt rapidly to changes in the business environment while remaining productive and efficient.

Most of the organizations that were successful during the 20th century were built like supertankers, and many of them still are. They have been used to enter new markets and crush their competitors by their sheer size, slowly moving forward following a course that the top management team set out long before the ship left harbor. Hubris usually follows with size and makes them blind and unable to adapt to their environment.

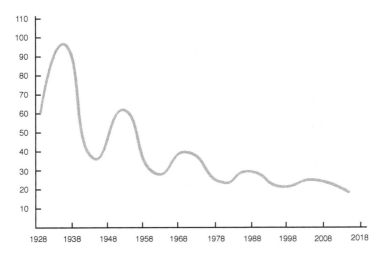

Figure 1: Average lifetime of S&P 500 companies (The Shift Index, Deloitte's Center for the Edge)

Now suddenly, these organizations might need to turn on a dime. Recent examples that had to do this, and failed, are Nokia and Kodak. Eighty-seven percent of the Fortune 500 firms in 1955 were gone in 2011, and life expectancy of a Fortune 500 company has decreased from 75 years, half a decade ago, to only 15 years; and is expected to decrease even more in the years ahead (Chew, 2012). This development is illustrated in figure 1.

THE HIERARCHIC CONTROL SYSTEM STILL PREVAILS

In reality, we never work in isolation. The work we do as individuals is directly or indirectly interdependent with the work other people do. To achieve our shared goals as an organization, each one of us needs to do the right things in the right way, and we must also coordinate our work efficiently and effectively.

To make this coordination easier, organizations establish and maintain various structures such as the hierarchical organization, processes, and projects. During the 20th century, the hierarchical organization solved the coordination challenges that organizations faced.

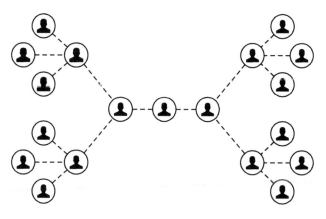

Figure 2: The hierarchical organization is a hub-and-spoke network

So how does this solution work? Technically, a hierarchical organization is a network, as illustrated in figure 2. If you look at it from the top, it is a so called 'hub and spoke' network, arranged like a chariot wheel, in which all traffic moves along spokes connected to the hub at the center.

The hierarchical organization was originally designed as a command hierarchy where people carry out orders given from the top of the hierarchy. Commands, tasks, and goals flow downwards in the hierarchy, from superiors to their subordinates. The results flow in the other direction, from the subordinates to their superiors ("Hierarchic Control System", 2015).

In a traditional hierarchical organization, most of the guidance and processes about the management and operation of the enterprise is typically produced and aggregated at the top. It is then cascaded down the hierarchy. The information must often pass each level of management on its way down until it reaches the intended receivers. Every level becomes an 'information tollgate' that has the responsibility and mandate to communicate the relevant information to appropriate receivers further down in the structure. In doing so, they can often select which people they think should receive the information, how they should receive it, when they should receive it, and exactly what they should receive.

THE HIERARCHICAL ORGANIZATION HAS WEAKNESSES

A major weakness of the hierarchical organization is related to how the structure is created and evolves. It determines an organization's ability to quickly mobilize resources in new ways. Since the overall structure is centrally created and managed in a hierarchical organization, the structure becomes rigid and cannot be easily or rapidly changed to adapt to new conditions.

Changes in the structure of a hierarchical organization are typically implemented in re-organization projects. These not only consume a lot of time and resources from management, but they often also paralyze the workforce. The re-organization projects introduce a great amount of uncertainty. People cannot control or influence the situation. That makes it hard for most people to keep up 'business as usual'.

Another major weakness of the hierarchical organization is related to how information may flow within the hierarchy, affecting the ability to provide people with the right information in the right time. In theory, a hub and spoke network allows information to cascade across the network, from the central hub and outwards along the spokes. In practice, it rarely works like the theory. There's a high probability that information needed by an individual further down in the hierarchy does not reach them, or that something happens to it along the way, as illustrated in figure 3 below.

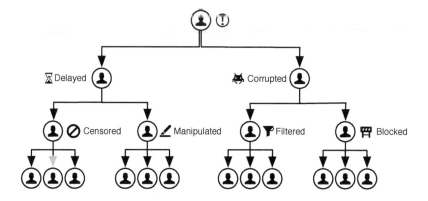

Figure 3: The fallacy of the hierarcical organization

To start with, it is hard for a manager to know exactly what information each individual subordinate needs, and thus potentially relevant information might be accidentally filtered out. Information might also be corrupted, censored, manipulated, delayed, or blocked as it is cascaded down the hierarchy.

Moreover, the flow of information is primarily one-directional. Formal rules, as expressed in policies, processes, and procedures steer how the information is intended or allowed to flow across the network. The flow is also determined by the behavior of the actors in the network who might – intentionally or unintentionally – filter, delay, manipulate, censor or even block the information from reaching the intended receivers.

The only way to get 'pure' information is to get direct access to the source. This is something that the hierarchical organization doesn't support by design. There are no formal links that connect people in different branches of the hierarchy directly to each other. If a person wants to exchange information with a person in another branch of the hierarchy, it might have to go all the way up in the hierarchy to where the two branches meet. This introduces transaction costs that limit the amount and frequency of communication between different parts of the organization.

INFORMAL NETWORKS ARE CRUCIAL IN ORGANIZATIONS

Informal networks have always been important, if not to say critical, for accessing information, collaborating, making decisions, and ensuring commitment to implement decisions. An informal network is a social network, a set of social ties between people, which exists within an organization, see figure 4.

Figure 4: Informal networks within an organization

Informal networks within organisations are different to the formal structures that perform these functions as they lack structure and arise spontaneously. They develop and change organically as people interact with new people and build bonds of trust between each other.

Informal networks are often seen as problematic as they bypass the formal structures for communication and decision-making, in a hidden way that cannot be controlled by management. Yet, most organizations would not function without them. A lot more information and knowledge flows through informal networks than through the formal organizational structures (Bryan, Matson &

Weiss, 2007). The informal networks have compensated for the lack of bandwidth, lateral connectivity, and inertia of the formal information flows that follow the hierarchical organization structure, by rapidly bringing new information to the awareness of both formal and informal decision-makers.

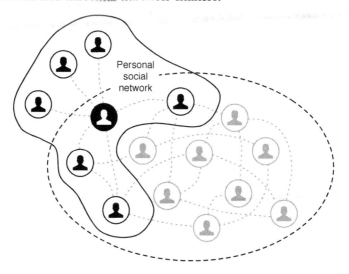

Figure 5: Personal social networks stretch beyond organizational borders

When we talk about *social networks* today, we typically refer to the social networks we have as individuals, with ourselves as the central hub. In contrast to informal networks, our personal social networks are not limited to the organization we work for. As illustrated in figure 5, they stretch far beyond the borders of an organization and include family, friends, ex-colleagues, online acquaintances, and other people we have some kind of relationship to. It doesn't have to be work-related. Yet our personal social networks are becoming more and more important for getting work done.

As knowledge workers, we use our personal social networks every day. We use them to find and get access to expertise and information, to discover and take action on opportunities, to solve problems, to get buy-in for decisions, and so on. They are especially important when we find ourselves in situations where we lack complete or accurate information to make decisions, or when faced with exceptions and problems we cannot handle on our own.

From an organizational perspective, employees' personal social networks allow the organization to get information from outside the organization, something that is critical in a rapidly changing world.

SOCIAL NETWORKS CAN BRIDGE STRUCTURAL HOLES

So-called *structural holes* appear in the flow of information between groups. If people are separated from each other by geography and organization, and are relatively unconnected (such as is often the case in a large organization), more structural holes will emerge.

Although the members of a group have strong ties to each other and exchange information with high velocity, much of the information exchanged within a group is redundant. New information and ideas must, by necessity, come from outside the group. The problem is that when the group members focus on their own goals and activities they communicate less with the world outside. They exchange less information with other groups. This phenomena is often called *groupthink*.

People's social networks can help an organization bridge its structural holes and reduce group-think (figure 6). If a member in a group has a social network with ties to people in other groups, then it can be used to access new and relevant information that the group otherwise wouldn't have access to.

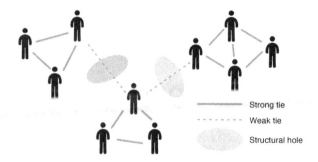

Strong tie
Weak tie
Structural hole

Figure 6: Social networks that stretch across groups help bridge structural holes

Depending on the size and structure of the social network it is more or less effective. When a social network becomes too dense and homogenous, it limits access to new information that represents other ideas, beliefs, and perspectives (see figure 7). The social network can easily turn into an echo chamber where the same information is shared and ideas are repeated over and over again, much like in a group that develops groupthink.

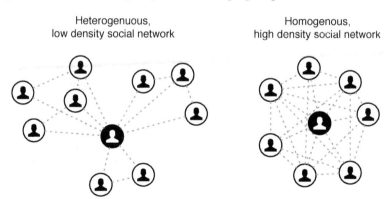

Figure 7: Different structure of social networks

Social networks often become dense and homogenous since people tend to develop relationships with people like themselves. If people are socially similar, they are also likely to have more shared interests. When people pursue their interests, they spend time at the same places as other people who share the same interests. When they meet, they communicate and develop relationships. If people are curious and open to new ideas and perspectives, it will likely benefit both themselves and the organizations they work for.

SOCIAL NETWORKS COMPLEMENT THE HIERARCHY

Social networks also compensate for the weaknesses – the inertia and inefficient information flows – that characterize the traditional hierarchical organization.

To begin with, the structure of a social network is flat. Its structure made up of a set of actors with interpersonal ties. The network grows and changes organically, taking any possible shape without being restricted by any formal rules, and with no central planning. New ties can be established as needed, without having to change the overall structure of the network.

In a social network, information can flow freely via the actors in the network, in any direction, across the interpersonal ties between the individuals in the network. These ties can be strong, weak, or absent.

While the velocity of the information exchange is greater where there are strong ties, more novel information is exchanged via the weak ties. It is the behavior of the actors in the network that entirely steers what information is exchanged as there are no formal rules for how the information may flow.

STRONG NETWORKS IMPROVE PERFORMANCE

A study from May 2009, surveying 3500 HR professionals, looked at how informal networks affect change in organizations and found that they had a major impact. A strong correlation was found between how successful a change initiative was and the strength of the initiative leaders' personal social networks. The majority of the less successful change initiatives were led by people described as having moderate or weak personal social networks.

In contrast, 93 percent of the successful change initiatives were led by leaders with strong or very strong personal social networks (Townsend & Yeung, 2009).

Another study managed to infer the social networks of 400,000 employees within a large organization in the consulting industry by analyzing their email communication. The purpose was to assess how the employee's social networks impact the performance of both individuals and the organization as a whole. The researchers found that work performance depends highly on the topology of people's social network, such as structural diversity, as well as the human capital and status of the contacts in their social networks. It matters to whom you are connected. Having strong ties to powerful people also seems to correlate with higher revenue.

To ensure that a team is successful and the team members perform well, it is important that the social networks of the team members have the desired characteristics (Wu, Lin, Aral & Brynjolfsson, 2009).

THE SOCIAL NETWORK IS THE NEW EXPERT

The hierarchical organization has not only been used to aggregate decision-making, to steer information flows, and to control execution, but also to aggregate knowledge and expertise to specific individuals. As a solution for building and providing access to knowledge in a large organization, the hierarchy had obvious advantages, the most important one being findability. Everyone knew who these experts were, and they could easily be located in the organizational chart. These *formally appointed* experts also used to act as hubs, or what Malcolm Gladwell calls Connectors. They helped to connect people and expertise across the workforce (Gladwell, 2000).

The world was stable and uncomplicated enough for the expert to provide most of the answers. Their positions as experts gave them much power and influence and, like any other power, it could be used for good and for bad. If nothing else, the experts enjoyed job security.

In today's fast moving, complex, and changing world, this way of aggregating knowledge and expertise has become a problem instead of a solution. The experts have become bottlenecks. People need faster access to more, broader, and deeper knowledge and expertise. The experts can't possibly build, keep, or access all the knowledge and expertise they need to provide to the rest of the workforce.

It is relatively easy to see how these experts become bottlenecks when there is a need to speed up and broaden the flow of information. Furthermore, all the knowledge that exists within an organization cannot be captured, aggregated, and maintained by a few select individuals. Much of the knowledge is tacit, and the vast majority of knowledge and expertise is distributed and hidden in the people's heads.

At a point in time, many seemed to think that an organization's knowledge could be captured and stored in databases. They also believed that employees would give it up for free, making the effort to record it on top of their daily workload. But history has shown this was nothing but management's dream.

Being an expert is no longer about pretending to know everything within a certain domain. It is about being part of a network of people, readily sharing what you know, being able to ask the right questions, and having the skills and the network to find the answers.

This shift from formal experts to expert networks makes the hierarchical organization even less relevant.

INNOVATION HAPPENS AT SOCIAL CROSSROADS

In an organization you never know when or where innovation will happen, where ideas will pop up, or where they will come to life. Innovation often happens at 'social crossroads'; places where people coming from different directions might meet, share their ideas, and perhaps develop and implement an idea.

More often than not, innovation is a by-product of a process, or something that happens seemingly *ad hoc*, rather than being the output of a pre-defined and highly repeatable process. The most fruitful meetings are often those that are spontaneous and unplanned, and where different ideas and perspectives collide. Nothing might happen, or anything might happen.

Our ability to access new information, knowledge, and ideas depends highly on our social capital; the resources our contacts hold, and the structure of our social network. The contacts are the people whom we can reach while the structure is how we can reach them.

Unlike financial capital, social capital is something owned by both parties in a relationship together. If the relationship ends, the social capital is dissolved. One party can't take it and walk away with it. As Steven Johnson expressed it, "chance favors the connected mind" (Riverhead Books, 2010).

The problem is that if we don't get the chance to meet new people, then those sought-after moments of serendipity and fortunate 'knowledge accidents' will not occur.

We also know from a lot of research that diversity in any form, whether it is interests, gender, race, age or national origin, has a positive impact on decision-making and innovation, as well as on individual and organizational performance. If we are connected to people outside our own groups, then we might get access to new information that positively influences our own performance, or we might exchange ideas that might lead to innovations.

In this respect it makes sense to diversify our social networks, to strive for a less dense network, by exposing ourselves to new situations where we can meet and connect with people that don't share the same interests, beliefs, or preferences. This might help to shed a whole new light on our ideas, beliefs, experiences, knowledge, or information.

AN ORGANIZATION NEEDS TO GET THE BALANCE RIGHT

The traditional hierarchical organization has major weaknesses that need to be addressed. New and viable alternatives to the traditional hierarchical organization are emerging, such as the increasingly popular Holocracy. So should organizations abandon hierarchy entirely and replace it with a new organizational model? Or should they keep the hierarchical organization and change it so it becomes more like a social network?

There is no simple answer to this question. At a bare minimum, an organization needs to enable people to build and make use of their social networks and engage in communities to get work done. Just as processes and projects are complementary structures to the hierarchical organization, social networks and communities are complementary structures that bring certain capabilities.

There needs to be a harmonious balance between multiple structures – such as the hierarchical organization, processes, communities, and social networks. So far, too much focus and effort has been put on building and maintaining the hierarchical organization and processes. Far too little attention has been given to empowering employees to build and make effective use their own social networks. The same goes for empowering employees to build, facilitate and participate in communities across organizational groups and locations.

CHAPTER 2

BREAKING THE CURSE OF PHYSICAL PROXIMITY

"Physical separation from others in daily life drastically reduces the likelihood of voluntary work collaboration."

Kiesler & Cummings, 2002

If you have ever worked for a startup or small company that grew, you have most likely experienced what happens when a company grows beyond a few dozen people.

First, people get divided into separate organizational groups so they can focus on their specialty areas, for example, to work with a specific customer or a specific business process. This means they now have a lot in common with the colleagues in their own group, and less in common with colleagues in other groups.

Suddenly people find themselves mostly talking to the colleagues in their own organizational group and close proximity. It's not that they don't want to talk to other colleagues, but talking to a colleague in another team requires them to invest time and energy to walk those extra steps (figure 8).

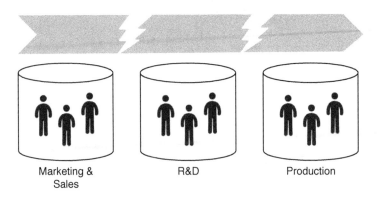

Marketing &   R&D   Production
Sales

Figure 8: As a company grows it becomes siloed

Then, as the company grows even more, the distance increases not to other colleagues but to the customers as well. Sales people and customer service personnel take care of the interaction with the customers so that other employees can focus on their work without being "disturbed" by customers.

To make the company more cost-efficient and profitable, more and more of the interaction with the customers is being automated with digital technology. The customers get less visible and more distant.

The further away from the customers people are, the more they tend to focus their time and energy on things that don't create any value for the customer; politics, climbing the career ladder, who reports to whom, inventing new roles, fighting to protect their positions. Inside out thinking and silo mentality slowly begin to take over.

In the light of this it makes perfect sense why IKEA, a widely successful company, has a policy that every employee that doesn't work at a store has to work for a few days every year in an IKEA store. They get to meet the customers.

After a few days in the trenches, they return to their regular job positions with real-world experience from IKEA's core business. They have experienced first-hand what challenges the store personnel face when meeting and serving customers. They can bring that experience into their own work. They understand better what they can do themselves to make the core business even more successful. Most important, they never lose sight of the customer and that serving and providing value to the customer is their reason for existence.

Although this is a great idea, it requires people to be physically closer to the customer. They also have to put their other tasks and responsibilities on hold for a few days. And anyway it is just for a few days per year. The rest of the year people spend at their offices, working and interacting mostly with people like themselves. It is hard to remain focused on the customer.

BIGGER ISN'T ALWAYS BETTER

There is a widespread assumption or belief that large organizations are more efficient than small organizations because they can enjoy economies of scale. That is, they obtain cost advantages due to their scale of operation, with cost per unit of output decreasing with increasing scale. But there are also diseconomies of scale. As illustrated in figure 9, diseconomies of scale occurs when an organization expands beyond its optimum scale (Q).

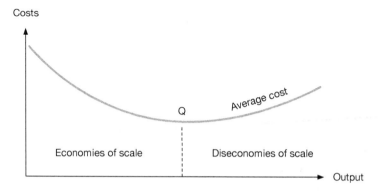

Figure 9: From economies to diseconomies of scale

Diseconomies of scale can be caused by internal reasons, such as:

- Poor communication due to organizational silos that stop information from flowing between different parts of the organization.
- Coordination problems due to the complexity and large number of resources involved in a large organization.
- Lower employee engagement that in turn leads to lower productivity per employee.
- The principal-agent problem where decision-making is appointed to managers who focus on their goals instead of the goals of the organization.

For knowledge-intensive organizations operating in an uncertain and rapidly changing environment, diseconomies of scale such as these are likely to appear early on in the organization's growth curve.

Economies of scale created by the ability to share technical infrastructure, consolidation of administrative functions, or savings from purchasing in bulk or receiving volume discounts can easily become overshadowed by costs related to efforts that aim to compensate for poor communication and coordination of resources.

Other and potentially more fatal diseconomies of scale, especially for an organization that operates in a highly competitive and rapidly changing business environment, are lower innovation and agility.

The bigger an organization gets, the harder it becomes to know people who work for the organization as well as to communicate and collaborate with them. This has a negative impact on employee productivity.

A study of 475 large publicly noted US companies in nine different industry sectors looked at the profit per employee as a productivity measure and plotted it against the number of employees for all the companies. It found a clear downward trend between employee productivity and number of employees. The more employees, the lower the productivity per employee. When employee numbers grow by 10 percent, you lose 1 percent productivity (Engelhardt, 2006).

Size also has a negative effect on employee engagement. If you work for a small organization it is likely that you are more engaged than if you work for a large organization. Research shows that the smallest companies have the most engaged employees. In organizations of ten and fewer employees, 42 percent of the employees reported that they were engaged at work. This is a huge difference compared to only 27 percent to 30 percent of the employees working at organizations with a thousand or more employees (Gallup, 2015).

It is feasible to assume that this has to do with the lack of communication between different parts of the organization that is caused by organizational and geographical silos.

POOR COMMUNICATION GENERATE COSTS

Efficient and effective communication has always been a challenge for organizations. Bad decisions, delayed projects, disengaged employees, duplicated work, and rework can be blamed on poor communication. The bigger and more dispersed an organization, the more common and the more severe the consequences of poor communication usually become.

The importance of successful communication to any joint endeavor cannot be overstated. All other factors being equal, an endeavor will be more likely to succeed the more and better people communicate with each other. If one wants to improve any aspects of how an enterprise is being managed and operated, one needs to start by improving the foundation: communication.

So what is communication then? Well, technically speaking it is the process of transmitting a message, consisting of symbols, that carries some meaning from a sender to a receiver. For the communication to be successful, the message needs to be interpreted and understood by the receiver.

The message is communicated through a channel. There are word-based communication methods such as speaking and writing, as well as non-verbal communication methods such as gestures, facial expressions, behaviors, and touch. These methods can be used in an immediate fashion in real life, or through some medium such as radio, television, or computers.

It often makes sense to distinguish between synchronous and asynchronous communication. Synchronous communication takes place in real-time, for example when two people have a conversation face-to-face, over instant messaging, or over the phone. Both the sender and recipient is present when the message is sent, which isn't the case for asynchronous communication.

Asynchronous communication, such as when we communicate via documents or emails, is often more challenging than synchronous communication. For example, the sender can get no immediate confirmation from the sender that the recipient has understood the message. Nor can the recipient immediately request additional information from the sender if the recipient found something in the message unclear or incomplete.

The purpose of communication is to fulfill some need of those involved, such as getting the receiver to do something, to get information back in return, to evoke some feeling, or to develop the relationship. Rich communication often requires some kind of interaction – a dialog or conversation – whereby each new communication builds upon previous communications. When people have ongoing interactions to pursue a shared goal, they are in fact collaborating (see figure 10).

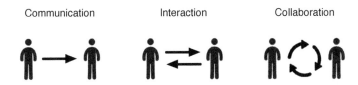

Figure 10: From communication and interaction to collaboration

Collaboration is the ongoing interaction between two or more people that pursue a single shared goal, for example a team working together in a project to develop a product.
The term cooperation is often used interchangeably with collaboration. But there is a subtle yet important difference. Cooperation is the ongoing interaction between two or more people that work on the same thing but who might be pursuing *different goals*, or pursuing the same goal but with *different motivations*.

Communication is the foundation for all types of human-to-human interaction and thereby also for cooperation and collaboration. If the communication is poor, a collaboration effort will be less likely to succeed. Conversely, if the communication is efficient and effective, a collaboration effort is more likely to succeed.

BEING CLOSE MAKES ALL THE DIFFERENCE

In 1977, when Massachusetts Institute of Technology professor Tom Allen published the results of his study of the communication among engineers in a research and development (R&D) facility, he presented overwhelming evidence that R&D effectiveness would increase if the communication between groups within the organization increased. Allen (1997) found that the interaction with people outside the team is the most important to performance, especially for complex projects where the team could not perform without getting new information from the outside world. Access to external information is highly correlated with performance.

For example, when a person lets the structure of the organization instead of the needs of the work determine the communication (communicating only with the people in their organizational group), they will not perform as well as someone who seeks information outside the group and develops contacts throughout the whole organization. Performance is affected both by how many people outside a team a person communicates with as well as by the amount of communication taking place.

Allen also studied how architecture influenced communication and how distance influenced the probability that two engineers would have weekly communication with each other. Although one can expect the amount of communication to decrease as the physical distance increases, the decrease in communication frequency that Allen found was dramatic. After only 25 to 30 meters, the likelihood that two engineers would have weekly communication dropped from 30 percent when they are a few meters apart to only 5 percent. If they were further away from each other, the probability remained around 5 percent (figure 11).

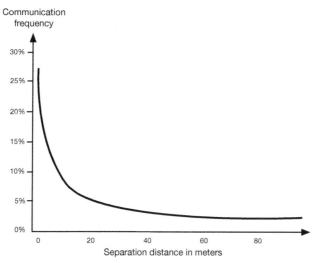

Figure 11: Physical distance and the probability of having frequent communication

Allen found that people almost only have frequent communication with people that are sitting within 25-30 meters. If they belong to the same organizational group, the probability will be higher, but the correlation between communication frequency and physical distance will remain the same. Unless people see a clear return of investment from taking a 30 meters walk to talk to someone, they will most likely not do so. And if they do, it doesn't matter if the person is 35 meters away or 20 kilometers. They primarily communicate and collaborate with people in close proximity and with people they already know or share a common task or goal with. It doesn't matter if they, as Allen found evidence for, would achieve better results if they worked with people outside their local environment or organizational groups.

In 1998, Bell Communications Research and University of Arizona published the results of a similar study that looked at the role of communication and physical proximity in scientific research collaboration. Like Allen, they found that physical proximity had a strong effect on the collaboration between researchers. They also found that this effect was independent from other factors such as if the researchers belonged to the same or different departments. For example, two researchers that belonged to different departments but were situated on the same floor were six times more likely to collaborate than two researchers that were situated on different floors or in different buildings, even if the latter belonged to the same department (figure 12).

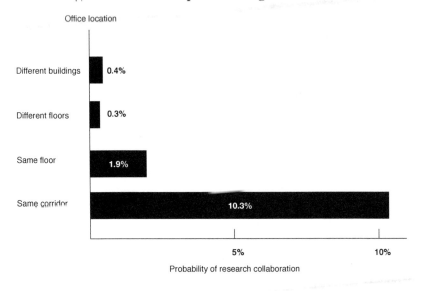

Figure 12: The probability of research collaboration

Physical proximity clearly impacts the likelihood of two people communicating with each other and thereby also the likelihood that they will start collaborating with each other. But there are other factors at play beyond just the frequency of communication, such as the quality of the communication. If people have high-quality communication (two-way communication involving multiple senses) it makes them more prone to collaborate. What starts as a general discussion might develop into more focused conversations about particular subjects or projects, eventually leading to collaboration.

Being physically close to each other also means that the transaction costs for communicating is low. When the physical distance increases, these costs increase. Informal communication becomes less economical. One would want to know in advance that the effort would pay off to invest the time and energy required to walk to another floor or building. But it's hard to know the value of an informal conversation in advance. As humans, we try to make rational choices, comparing the costs and benefits of certain actions. Since most people are risk-averse, they would likely stay at their desks even if there is a good chance that the walk will benefit them.

THE PROBLEM OF SCALING COMMUNICATION

The existence of structural holes and groupthink can explain many of the communication problems that large or dispersed organizations suffer from. These are in turn consequences of the difficulty to communicate efficiently and effectively as an organization grows.

The increasingly complex and interdependent nature of work requires more people to be involved and contribute. The problem is that conversations where a lot of people participate and interact with each other easily become messy. Even in a face-to-face meeting with just a few people, a discussion can easily get out of hand. To illustrate this, let's take a look at figure 13.

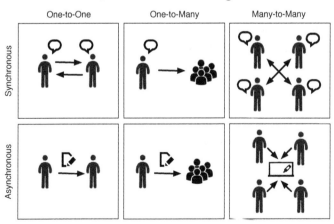

Figure 13: Different ways of communicating

One-to-one interaction is the simplest form of interaction. As we move to one-to-many interaction, it becomes trickier and potentially messier.

A typical example is where a person shares some information and asks the recipients for feedback. Collecting the feedback from many people at once and putting it together is usually a cumbersome task if each person provides the feedback individually. If they had provided the feedback together, they could have made it much easier for the person requesting the feedback. But this would have required them to have a many-to-many interaction, which is the hardest type of interaction.

The challenges of scaling communication present themselves at relatively small numbers of participants. Anyone who has been part of a rapidly growing small organization should be able to testify to this. When the organization grows beyond a few dozen people, it becomes hard to interact frequently with everyone. You definitely can't meet everyone for an informal chat at the water cooler. This in turn limits your ability to know what is going on, to get to know colleagues, and to exchange information and experiences with them. Many-to-many communication just doesn't scale as the organization grows.

To overcome this, organizations have traditionally established formal one-to-many communication that follows the organizational structure. Many-to-many communication is allowed to happen only within smaller organizational groups and teams. It becomes the responsibility of management to communicate and exchange information between other organizational groups. This way, communication chaos can be avoided. However, this solution doesn't work well in a constantly changing and unpredictable environment where work is highly interdependent and non-routine.

PHYSICAL PROXIMITY WINS EVERY TIME

If you are physically close to someone, it is likely that you will frequently communicate. Over time, you will get to know each other, perhaps even like each other. You develop trust in each other. When you do, you are more likely to share your ideas with each other instead of keeping them for yourselves. Trust creates room for spontaneity, for ideas to flow freely. Being physically close allows you to communicate almost effortlessly, with high quality, about even trivial things. No structure or constraints need to be imposed to the communication processes; ideas can be exchanged immediately as they pop up in your heads.

The more steps you have to walk, the more doors you have to open, and the more doorkeepers you have to pass to talk to someone, the less likely it is that you will make the effort. It certainly won't happen spontaneously, frequently, or be about trivial things - such as what you like to eat for lunch or what you do in your spare time. Chances are you won't get to know this person. You won't develop trust in each other. You won't exchange ideas freely with each other. If you come up with an idea, and this person is the one that can make it reality, you probably won't know that. Anyway, it won't happen. A potential innovation dies before it got a chance to live.

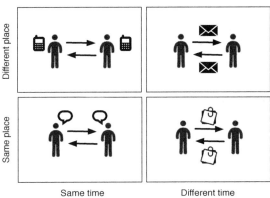

Figure 14: Communication technology is needed when separated by time and/or space

As illustrated in figure 14, when people are separated by time and/or distance, people need to use some kind of technology to communicate with each other when separated by space and/or time. When separated by space and not time, they need a synchronous (real-time) communication technology such as telephony to communicate. When separated by time but not space, the need an asynchronous communication tool, which can be as simple as leaving a note at the person's desk. When separated by both time and space, they need an asynchronous communication tool that transfers the message across space. Before we had digital communication tools such as email, people had to write each other letters sent by regular (snail) mail.

When it comes to communication efficiency and effectiveness, nothing can replace face-to-face communication when people are separated by neither time nor space. Face-to-face communication is the natural way for humans to communicate and the bandwidth of this communication is huge. Only 7 percent of this communication consists of words and 93 percent consists of visual cues such as body language, eye, and vocal cues such as the pitch and tone of voice (Gallo, 2007).

CREATING VIRTUAL PROXIMITY

Of course, we can't all sit next to each other, in the same room, or even in the same building. The number of people involved in many enterprises makes this impossible, and many organizations also need to be present at multiple locations.

Traditionally, when people have been geographically separated and needed to meet, they would travel to the same location for a face-to-face meeting. But this is too costly for most organizations today. Most of the costs are associated with traveling, such as unproductive traveling time, monetary and environmental costs of traveling, mental stress and exhaustion due to time zone adjustments and lack of sleep, and social consequences of being away from our friends and family.

All these things and more make traveling something most people like to avoid unless it is necessary. So they have to find alternate and more powerful ways to communicate when people are separated by time and/or space.

In addition, to address many of the challenges that organizations face they need to help people communicate more and better. Better communication methods help people access and act on new information quicker, coordinate actions faster and better across a large and dispersed workforce. Ideas can be assessed and acted upon no matter where they come from.

It is a well-known fact that small companies are more innovative than large companies. A small company is also more agile and more responsive to customer needs, and collaboration tends to happen (Intuit, 2010). This is obviously related to how people in a small company can be physically close to each other as well as to customers, allowing them to communicate frequently, effortlessly. The only way for a large and distributed organization to become a bit more like a small company is to create *virtual proximity* between people with the use of digital communication technology.

Virtual proximity is created when digital communication technologies make it really easy for people to have frequent, rich, spontaneous, and informal conversations with each other, no matter where they are physically located. It makes the perceived distance between people shrink, making it seem that participants are physically close to each other. Organizations need to create a digital work environment where it is as easy for people to digitally communicate, interact, and collaborate, as if located in the same room.

CHAPTER 3

ADAPTING
TO A NEW
BUSINESS REALITY

*"Techhology is shifting the power
away from the editors, the publishers,
the establishment, the media elite.
Now it's the people who are in control."*

*Rupert Murdoch
Australian American business magnate*

Imagine looking into the living room of a suburban middle-class family in the US in the '60s. The family is gathered around the television, and so are most likely the neighbors' families. It is Saturday evening and they are watching a popular television show. In the break, there are some commercials; this is how they get to know about new products and services. They watch television, read the newspaper, or are exposed to advertisements when driving.

The more marketing space a company can buy in these broadcasting media, and the more powerful brand message they are able create, the more they will influence people to buy their product or service. If a neighbor or a colleague buys a new product and talks well about it, it is likely they will buy the product themselves. But they won't get to hear many other people's opinions. Most of the influence will come from the people they already know, often people in their close proximity. So if Coca-Cola dominates the space for fizzy drinks and most colleagues and friends buy Coca-Cola, it is likely the family will drink Coca-Cola and not some other carbonated beverage from an obscure or lesser known brand.

Let's move on to today. A fundamental shift is happening regarding how consumers become aware and make up their minds about products and services. Markets are no longer created and controlled with broadcast marketing. It is becoming less common that people buy a product just because they have seen an ad on TV or in the newspaper. They get to know about a new product from many media, increasingly from digital media and social media. When people try to make up their minds about a product, before they make any buying decision, they prefer to look to other people similar to themselves. In fact, most people trust those they consider to be like themselves more than they trust advertising and organizations – even if they don't know the person in question.

On the Internet, they can now find and connect with people like themselves all over the world. They are no longer limited to the people in their close proximity, or to existing ties such as family members, friends, colleagues, or neighbors. They can connect with anyone, and anyone can be an influencer. Most of the media where they get to know about the product isn't one-way or controlled by the company that offers the product. Instead they can discuss the product with other people who have bought the product, are thinking of buying the product, or have bought a similar product from a competitor.

The Internet, increased connectivity, and affordable and easy-to-use digital communication devices and tools have made this shift possible. The new digital communication technologies are changing the rules of the game in fundamental ways:

- The power of communication is being democratized and distributed to everyone, instead of being owned and controlled by a few
- Information can flow freely without being gated, filtered, or distorted
- The technology treats everybody as equals when it comes to their right to make their voices heard.

The bottom line is that companies are no longer in charge of the communication process with consumers. The power is shifting from companies to consumers. It is a radical shift and many companies are not prepared at all. The question they have to ask now is, how do we adapt to a reality where the customer is in control?

THIS IS THE END OF THE INDUSTRIAL CORPORATION

The rapid development of new digital communication technology is changing the world as we know it. It changes our society, companies, and entire industries. It changes the way we think and behave as individuals, consumers and employees. The fundamental driver is that the cost of communicating has collapsed. As a result, the power of communication has been democratized and made available to nearly everyone.

We can now connect with anyone from anywhere in the world to exchange information, ideas, and experiences. It is now possible to interact and collaborate with people at a greater scale, lower cost, and smaller effort than ever. People from across the world can team up, as author Clay Shirky expressed it, to "collaborate with a birthday party's informality and a multinational's scope".

The purpose of the traditional industrial corporation was, according to the Anglo-American economist and Nobel Prize winner, Ronald Coase, to bring together all resources needed for an enterprise under one roof and one management. This helped to reduce the transactional costs, especially the communication costs. The traditional industrial corporation was designed the way it was due to high transaction costs, and high communication costs in particular. Since digital communication technology lowers these costs, it opens up a world of opportunities regarding how companies can be designed, operated and managed. The modern corporation emerges (figure 15).

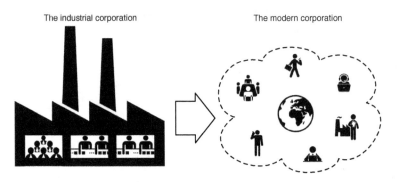

Figure 15: The industrial corporation is being replaced

This is a great opportunity for new companies, and a huge threat to existing companies that were designed based on the idea of the industrial corporation.

As an example, in 2015 Amazon overtook the position from Walmart as the largest US retailer by market capitalisation. Amazon is driving the change in how people shop, from physical stores to online, while at the same time using digital technology to be smaller and more nimble as an organization than Walmart. As a comparison, Amazon has grown at almost 30 percent per year since 2010 while Walmart has stopped growing (Hartung, 2015).

We don't know where the digitalization and democratization of communication will take us and how it will change things. Not until many years from now, will we be able to look back and map the course of this shift. According to Amara's law, we overestimate the effects of a technology in the short run and underestimate the effects in the long run. We know this is true if we think about the printing press, telephony, email, and basically every new communication technology introduced in society. When each of these technologies were introduced, people were either skeptical to the new technology, or they expected too much from it. Surely the change and impact wasn't huge in the beginning. But today we can see that they have fundamentally changed our attitudes and behaviors as individuals and of society as a whole.

CONSTANT CHANGE IS THE NEW NORMAL

The business environment most companies operate in is anything but static. It's changing faster and faster, and in new ways; it's becoming more and more unpredictable. This means that organizations can't do long-term planning the way they used to. Instead they have to prepare themselves for change and make sure they can adapt to new conditions and situations (figure 16).

When trying to achieve this, they soon become aware of the conflict between agility and productivity. How can they maintain or even increase efficiency and productivity when they need to adapt to new conditions all the time?

The traditional industrial corporation was designed to produce as much of the same thing as fast and as cost-efficient as possible.

The systems needed to operate and manage an enterprise were designed for optimization: management practices; organizational structure; performance systems; IT systems. As a result, companies have evolved into machine-like constructs that are as stale as they are efficient.

Now, suddenly, they need to regain the abilities they lost during that transformation:'

- Their ability to be close to their customers and responsive to their changing needs
- Their ability to adapt to new market conditions
- Their ability to innovate
- Their ability to build and make use of new relationships with partners and suppliers.

Companies might even need to change the foundation they were built on: their business model. This is hard even for a small start-up. How can a large and dispersed company, optimized for efficiency and growth, change so radically?

Yet this seismic shift is a reality they must prepare for. When it happens they have to adapt. What if another company produces the things the company produces faster, cheaper, and even better? What if someone innovates or invents a new product that serves the needs and wants of customers better than its product does? What if someone creates an experience that wins the hearts and minds of the company's customers? How will the company stand a chance to win them back when focused on producing the same stuff cheaper and faster? It needs to change the machine. It needs to redesign the machine to create new or different things, in new ways.

The paradox is that only people can change the machine. It takes skilled, talented, creative, and passionate people. Not people that have been trained to follow procedures and comply with rules. A community of creative, talented, and engaged people is the foundation of any company that wants to survive and thrive in the long run.

THE DIMINISHING RETURNS OF OPTIMIZATION

During the last couple of decades, many companies have outsourced or sold parts of their business that other companies could do faster, better, cheaper. Outsourcing allowed them to focus on their core business: the things that made them unique or they believed they could do better than other companies, such as R&D and marketing. It all goes in line with what Peter F. Drucker once said, that marketing and innovation produce results and that all the rest are costs. As an example, Apple's widely successful products are designed and marketed by Apple in California, US, but manufactured by companies all over the world. Apple employs around 80 000 people, but over 200 000 workers in 100 production lines are involved in just the production of the iPhone 6 (Lovejoy, 2014). Few of these are employed by Apple.

Products and services also become more and more commoditized, so the differentiating factor that makes a customer choose a product and brand over another is customer experience – the perceived value generated by all interactions with a brand and its products and services. The customer experience will determine the success or failure of the brand and its products and services. Companies able to create new value for customers, or even create new markets by creating new needs, will be the winners. The only way to escape the curse of commoditization is to become a game-changer. Again, Apple can serve as an example. They disrupted the music industry with the iPod and iTunes, and later the mobile phone industry with the iPhone and the PC market with the iPad. By being a game-changer, introducing new product categories as well as leading the innovation within their existing product categories such as smartphones, Apple are able to take 90% of the profits in the smartphone industry while having a market share of 'only' 17 percent.

Not only do the attitudes and behaviors of consumers change fast and in unpredictable ways. Consumers increasingly want to interact with companies and be served via digital channels. To adapt to this new reality where the power is shifting from companies to consumers, companies will need to rethink everything from how they design systems and processes to their business models – taking the consumers as their starting point.

The companies that excel both at understanding consumers and collaborating to turn these insights into new innovations, will lead the development in their industries and earn most of the profit. They won't be able do that simply through optimizing their processes and operations.

COLLABORATION WILL FUEL PRODUCTIVITY

When companies focus more on innovation and marketing, they also face new challenges. Collaborative and complex problem solving is the essence of many employees' work today, and they need to be empowered to do this as well as possible. Problematically, strategies and methods used to automate and optimize routine work can't be applied to non-routine knowledge work.

To start with, non-routine knowledge work is often interdependent. When people collaborate on routine work it can often be described and orchestrated as a process that can be repeated over and over again. We don't even think about it as collaboration. Non-routine work, such as turning ideas into new products and solving problems, is a different story. We rarely know in advance who should collaborate with whom and how. People need to collaborate more freely and spontaneously than is the case for routine work, deciding with whom to collaborate and how as they go along. To achieve ad hoc collaboration, people need to be creative and self-propelled, and have great communication and collaboration skills.

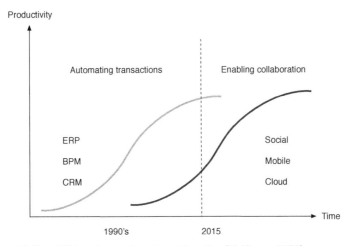

Figure 16: The shift from transactions to collaboration (McKinsey, 2009)

Furthermore, they need to have tools and ways of working that empower them. Companies need to support this kind of collaboration if they are to stand a chance of improving productivity, innovation and organizational responsiveness. This is also why collaboration must be seen as their new productivity frontier. To exploit this productivity potential, companies need to make use of new digital communication technologies that enable collaboration across all barriers (see figure 16).

To deal with the increasing complexity, speed of change and uncertainty companies face, they must master and excel at collaboration. Unfortunately, many executives and decision-makers don't make the connection between collaboration and market success. They forget that collaboration is the reason an organization exists in the first place. They need to be reminded that it's sole purpose is to bring together people with certain talent, skills, and expertise to work together on a specific enterprise.

CHAPTER 4

UNDERSTANDING THE CHANGING NATURE OF WORK

*"We have to undo a one hundred-year-old concept
and convince our managers that their role is not to control people
and stay 'on top' of things,
but rather to guide, energize and excite."*

*Jack Welch
CEO of General Electric 1981-2001*

In 1959 management guru Peter F. Drucker coined the term knowledge worker and defined it as "one who works primarily with information or one who develops and uses knowledge in the workplace" (Drucker, 1959).

Knowledge workers are those of us who contribute our knowledge, who 'think for a living'. Typical examples are software developers, architects, communication specialists, engineers, and lawyers. Knowledge work is about such things as solving problems, investigations, research, creating content, interacting and communicating with other people, and so on.

For many employees today, so called knowledge work makes up the majority of their work. The Work Foundation estimated that we have a 30-30-40 workforce in the developed world; 30 percent work in jobs with high knowledge content, 30 percent work with some knowledge content, and 40 percent are in jobs with less knowledge content (Brinkley, Fauth, Mahdon & Theodoropoulou, 2009). This is illustrated in figure 17.

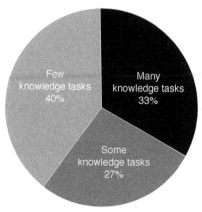

Figure 17: The 30-30-40 knowledge economy workforce

Being a knowledge worker isn't the same thing as being a white-collar worker, or office worker if you like. Most blue-collar workers have some knowledge content in their jobs. As more and more routine work becomes automated, the amount of knowledge work that blue-collar workers perform increases.

The basis of knowledge work is the knowledge of individuals rather than processes, procedures and manuals. It is reshaping the economy, with a whole new breed of companies and organizations emerging. Peter F. Drucker predicted knowledge work to become the basic means of production rather than capital, natural resources, or labor. In the 21st century, productivity and innovation will be the basis for value creation. This will make knowledge workers the leading social group in the knowledge society.

A SHIFT FROM ROUTINE TO NON-ROUTINE JOBS

Work is not only shifting from physical work to cognitive work, but also from routine work to non-routine work. This shift is the most dramatic one. A study of job polarization in the US shows that non-routine occupations have exploded (figure 18) since 1975 while routine occupations have seen a corresponding decline.

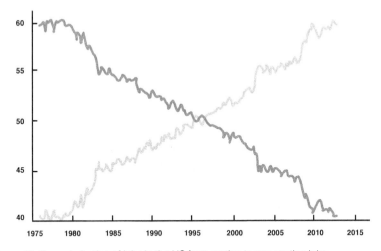

Figure 18: The polarization of jobs in the US from routine to non-routine jobs

This shift from routine to non-routine work applies to both manual tasks and cognitive tasks, i.e. knowledge work (Albanesi, Gregory, Patterson & Şahin, 2013). For example, routine tasks performed by doctors and nurses will become redundant when these can be automated or outsourced to the patients themselves using technology for self-examination. Software and articifial intelligence is taking over repetitive and routine-based knowledge work, just as robots are taking over repetitive and routine physical work in the factories (figure 19).

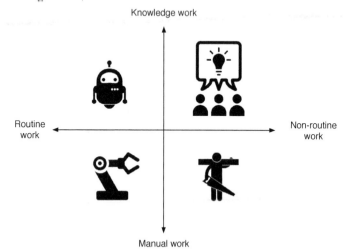

Figure 19: A larger part of the workforce perform knowledge non-routine work

We still need people to do manual non-routine tasks, such as the carpenter that builds a shelf at your house, or the wedding planner that organizes a wedding. Contrary to what one might think, non-routine physical work is in fact increasing. For example, Toyota is putting humans back into manufacturing so they can learn how to improve production lines and build better cars, faster: (*Trudell, Hagiwara & Bloomberg, 2014*)

UNUTILIZED PRODUCTIVITY POTENTIAL

Companies rely on a growing workforce of knowledge workers to innovate and market new products and services. At the same time, the benefits of optimization efforts, such as optimizing procurement processes or outsourcing supporting business functions, are diminishing. They have every reason to turn their improvement efforts towards knowledge work and collaboration. And there is definitely room for improvement.

A study by IDC claims that knowledge workers spend from 15 percent to 35 percent of their time just on searching for information; 15 percent of that time is spent on duplicating existing information.

More recent research by McKinsey (2012) supports the idea that there is much potential in improving knowledge work. Their conclusion is that the productivity of knowledge workers can increase with as much as 20 to 25 percent of companies successfully adopting social technologies to enhance communications, knowledge sharing, and collaboration. For example, they found that knowledge workers spend 28 percent of their workweek reading emails.

Let's try to imagine how a typical knowledge worker would spend a working week (figure 20)

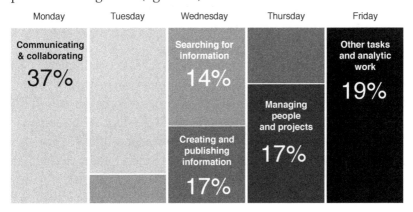

.Figure 20: The typical workweek of a knowledge worker

To begin with, the study by McKinsey estimates almost two days would go to communication and collaboration. Most of that time is used for reading and answering emails. Two days would be spent on an equal amount of searching for information, creating and sharing information, and coordinating activities. The remaining day would be spent on role-specific tasks – individually performed tasks that other people need not be directly involved in, such as data entry, content creation, and information analysis.

Birkinshaw and Cohen's (2013) research about productivity shows knowledge workers spend, on average, as much as 41 percent of their workday on activities that "offer little personal satisfaction and could be handled competently by others." They also found that knowledge workers, on their own, could increase their productivity by 20 percent, translating to one day per week by identifying low value tasks and either eliminating or delegating these tasks to someone else.

Eliminating or simplifying non-value adding tasks, such as administrative tasks, is an easy goal. It will also create win-win situations where the organization wins in terms of increased productivity and decreased costs and where the employee wins in terms of a more endurable and pleasant work situation. It will free up resources for improving communication and collaboration. To improve knowledge-based work, companies will need to use 'softer' strategies and methods than they used so far during the industrial era.

For example, when the role of technology was to automate manual tasks and remove the need for human labor, it wasn't as essential as it is today to design the technology to fit humans. If people wanted to keep their jobs, they had to adapt to the system. But this approach doesn't work with knowledge workers. They have to feel empowered and engaged to become more productive and innovative.

The work environment, including the tools knowledge workers need to get their work done, must be designed to fit with human nature and leverage collaborative human behaviors. Companies can only achieve this if they truly understand people and their needs in different situations. The problem is that traditional business development takes the company and its objectives as a starting point rather than the individual's. It focuses on such things as the organizational structure and processes, not the individual's tasks and situations. So, to improve the productivity of knowledge work, a company has to take the individual as a starting point and invest heavily in developing the employees and their work environment.

KNOWLEDGE WORK IS BECOMING FLUID

The inputs and outputs of knowledge work comprise information and knowledge; varying from time to time, from situation to situation. The purpose, activities, roles, and resources involved in knowledge work similarly vary.

A colleague of mine once said "I don't follow a process, I follow a cloud of activities". This is because it is hard or almost impossible to define the structure of knowledge work in advance. The structure emerges as the work proceeds. We are creating the process as we go along. To do that, we need to use our creativity, we need to look beyond the standard ways of practice, and we need to question things.

This is completely different working on a production line in a factory, where workers follow pre-defined and highly repeatable processes. Questioning rules is often out of the question as it has the potential to disrupt operations.

When people talk about business processes, they usually think about processes that are highly structured and repeatable, e.g. a manufacturing process. It is easy to describe the activities, their sequence, and the inputs and outputs of such a process. The same isn't true for a series of activities that seem to happen ad hoc, for example, when people solve a problem. Some don't even consider it to be a process. Yet, nothing in the definition of a process ('a series of actions or steps taken to produce something') says you must know the structure or output of the process beforehand, or that the process must be repeatable.

Rinde (2007) writes about the concepts of barely repeatable processes and easily repeatable processes. The latter refer to processes that are static and predictable. Industrial processes like supply, manufacturing, and distribution of goods would fall into this category. As would more transactional processes such as procurement and billing.

For easily repeatable processes, the process is often implemented, managed, and driven by IT systems, such as ERP (Enterprise Resource Planning) and PLM (Process Lifecycle Management) systems. These systems are, according to Rinde, "resource oriented, transactional, event driven systems". They can handle large volumes of events and transactions with great precision. They provide full control over the resources. Detailed procedures describe exactly how employees should carry out any tasks. Systems control the flow of activities. All this is possible because the processes are rigid and highly repeatable. The activities in the process and their structure is well known, and the expected output.

Let's take a purchasing process as an example of an easily repeatable process: a company is to purchase a product to be used as inputs in its own production processes. The company has an exact specification of the product, how many it needs, and when it needs them. It sends a request for proposal to a few selected suppliers and in response, the suppliers send their quotations. The company then reviews the quotations and sends a purchase order to the supplier that offers the best combination of price, availability and quality. The supplier delivers the ordered products, and the company receives and records the delivery. Finally the supplier sends an invoice to the company, and the company sends a payment after having checked the invoice against the delivery.

This process is easily repeatable. It can be used over and over again. The output of the process is specified and known in advance. The activities and workflow remains the same even if other products would be purchased. The process can be orchestrated end-to-end with an ERP system and many activities can be automated. Barely repeatable processes, on the other hand, comprise activities and tasks that employees spend most of their time performing. They often start with some kind of interaction, for example via email or a phone call. The output can rarely be defined in advance, and the activities and the structure of the process emerges as the activities and tasks are performed. Since the output and structure of the process cannot be defined in advance, such processes cannot be implemented and driven by systems. Instead, employees get a variety of tools that help them perform their tasks and coordinate resources, and activities as required. This puts a heavy responsibility on the individual to organize the process in a good way and to perform the right tasks in the right way.

If you work with "people" processes such as services and support, you know there is rarely one process that looks like the other. Every customer has a different issue or need, and serving it might require different resources, activities, and workflow. You will make phone calls, have meetings, search for information, collaborate with other people - things you didn't know you needed to do when the process started. The output, such as the solution of an issue, will differ from time to time. The total time and resources that a knowledge-intensive organization spends on these processes are likely larger than for easily repeatable processes. Rinde argues that most, as much as two thirds, of the value-creation in modern enterprises takes place in barely repeatable processes.

Much more is required from the people who take part in a barely repeatable process than an easily repeatable one. Instead of simply following instructions created by process engineers, instructions that to a large degree have been implemented in IT-systems, they have to be process engineers themselves and design the operation on the fly as they execute it. On top of this demand, the work environment is becoming more and more complex due to increased time pressure, mergers and acquisitions, telework, virtual teams, and many daily interruptions and interactions.

There is also a lot of waste in barely repeatable processes, and hence a lot of potential in improving on-the-fly operations. Even if a process is barely repeatable, there is often some repeatability for individual tasks. How we perform a certain task then becomes important. If we can perform each task with greater efficiency and effectiveness, the effects can be immense if we sum up all those tasks. How we perform tasks and the capabilities required to do so should be a high priority when improving knowledge work. In the digital realm, we must equip ourselves with the right tools that enable smarter ways of working to emerge.

EXCEPTIONS BECOME THE RULE

The increasing complexity and uncertainty that companies face also increases the number of exceptions they have to deal with. Besides, the exceptions are becoming harder to deal with. No manual or procedure can help employees deal with all exceptions. What rules we have are restrictive; in a dynamic and changing environment, rules are meant to be broken.

Patel (2010) sees working with exceptions as one of three modes of work: process, project, and exceptions (figure 21).

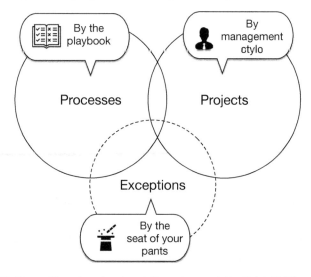

Figure 21: Three different modes of work (based on model by Patel, 2010)

According to Patel, for pre-defined processes, we can just follow the playbook. For projects, we can fall back upon our individual experience and established working methods for leading teams and collaborative efforts. But for the exceptions, each one is different and we need to handle it in its own special way. Here we have to fly by the seat of our pants. Be creative. Improvise. Try new things. Bend and break rules.

The focus on optimization in many companies makes them value highly structured and repeatable work higher than less structured and less repeatable work. In the name of optimization, they focus on automation, procedures, rules, and compliance. Unfortunately, it happens at the expense of creative work, problem solving, improvisation, innovation, and spontaneous collaboration.

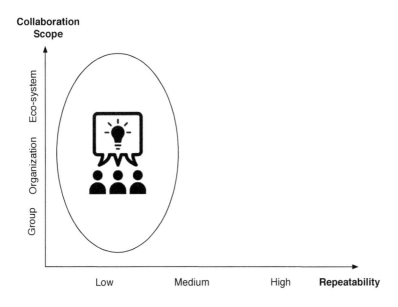

Figure 22: An increasing amount of knowledge work is non-routine and interdependent

As illustrated in figure 22, knowledge work isn't just shifting from routine to non-routine. It also requires more coordination and collaboration across groups since the work becomes more and more interdependent. This is a major challenge for knowledge workers.

CHAPTER 5

EMPOWERING
THE
EMPLOYEES

*"To escape the curse of commoditization,
a company has to be a game-changer,
and that requires employees who are proactive, inventive and zealous.
Problem is, you can't command people
to be enthusiastic, creative and passionate.
These critical ingredients for success in the creative economy
are gifts that people will bring to work
each day only if they're truly engaged."*

Dr Gary P. Hamel

Innovation is stalling. Productivity is, if not falling, not improving. It is hard to recruit and retain talent. People are leaving, or they want to leave, their jobs. We recognize these symptoms in all kinds of organizations, especially in large and distributed organizations. The patient is obviously not feeling well, but what is causing these symptoms? Much can be attributed to falling employee engagement.

So what do we mean by employee engagement? This definition from Wikipedia is as good as any:

> *"An 'engaged employee' is someone who is fully involved in, and enthusiastic about, his or her work, and thus will act in a way that furthers their organization's interests."*

As humans, we all need to feel part of something larger than ourselves, where we are somehow contributing to a common good. When we feel we do, we also become more motivated and our contributions will be greater. In the end, it will benefit us all as well as ourselves as individuals.

According to Gallup, an organization loses thousands of dollars per disengaged employee each year. Disengaged employees produce less and have more sick days than their more engaged colleagues. They also undermine the work of colleagues by passing on their cynicism and negativity to them (Gallup, 2002). A worldwide study of employee engagement from 2013 found that only 13 percent of employees are engaged at work. The majority of employees - 63 percent - are not engaged, which means they don't feel committed to their jobs and lack the motivation to contribute in positive ways to their organizations goals (Gallup, 2013). In the light of this, it is no surprise that senior leaders identify low employee engagement as one of the three biggest threats facing their business (Economist Intelligence Unit, 2010).

Multiple studies have proven that there is a strong correlation between employee satisfaction, customer satisfaction, and investor returns. The companies with the most engaged employees show significantly higher productivity than companies with the least engaged employees. Employees that are engaged are more focused and motivated. Also, they are less likely to be absent from work. As illustrated in figure 23, both these things lead to increased productivity (Insync Surveys, 2012).

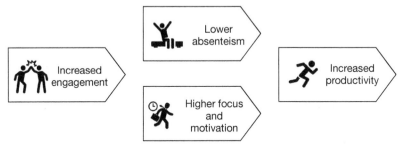

Figure 23: Increased engagement leads to increased productivity (Insync Surveys, 2012)

So why do so many employees feel disengaged? To answer that question, one needs to understand all the different ways that their work environment is changing. Their workload is increasing at the same time as employees are expected to produce more, faster and faster. The nature of work is changing. Employees find themselves working in more complex work environments. Mergers and acquisitions, frequent organizational changes, and new partnerships all contribute to change fatigue and the risk of overwhelming employees.

The work environment is also becoming more disconnected due to the globalization and the rise of working in virtual teams, outsourcing, and remote working. People are having more and more interactions with more – and often unknown – people. On top of all this, they need to quickly adapt to new conditions and at the same time be creative and innovative. The problem is that organizations haven't been designed to help them do this. Most organizations have been designed for efficiency and economies of scale, not for enabling collaboration, creativity, and personal responsibility. Too often, people feel like cogs in a big machine.

ORGANIZATIONS RUN ON THE WRONG ASSUMPTIONS

In his popular TED talk 'The surprising science of motivation' (2010), Daniel Pink talks about the mismatch that exists "between what science knows and what business does" when it comes to how organizations try to motivate their employees to perform better. The bottom line is that existing performance models in most organizations are built on extrinsic motivators – around carrots and sticks.

These models worked fine for the routine, left-brain, rule-based tasks of the 20th century, and since they worked fine previously, it seems intuitive that they will continue to work fine also in the 21st century. But as routine-based tasks have become increasingly easy to automate, or outsource to companies in developing countries, these kinds of jobs are disappearing at an increasing rate. The jobs that remain and the work that now has to be carried out in the companies in the developed world consist mostly of non-routine conceptual tasks, carried out by right-brained, creative, and rule-questioning people.

Science knows that *if-then* rewards, like bonuses and commissions, don't work for this kind of work. As a matter of fact, they often have the opposite effect than intended; the higher the extrinsic rewards, such as a bonuses, the worse performance can get. As an example, economists at the London School of Economics looked at 51 studies of pay-for-performance plans inside of companies and found that financial incentives can result in a negative impact on overall performance. ("Dan Pink: The puzzle of motivation", 2009)

Organizations are apparently making important decisions about their performance and their future based on the wrong assumptions because the stuff that motivates people doing right-brained work comes from within them. Their motivation isn't sparked by extrinsic rewards, only suffocated. What really incentivizes knowledge workers is to pursue a purpose, to have the freedom to control their our own situations, and to get the chance to get better and better at something. This is what Daniel Pink calls purpose, autonomy, and mastery. People that are truly passionate and dedicated to their work of course want a decent salary, but only so they don't have to think about money. They want to focus on doing their work, the way they see it best, and becoming better and better at it. For enhancing people's intrinsic motivation, recognition in terms of praise and feedback are much more fruitful than monetary.

WORK IS NO LONGER A PLACE

A lot of different technologies are available that make working from anywhere, a.k.a. mobile working, feasible and effective. Knowledge workers are being liberated from their desks by mobile technologies such as mobile broadband, smartphones, and cloud computing. Still, until recently, knowledge work used to be tied to a specific location, even computing. We are in the middle of the shift from working with a PC on a desk during office hours, to working from anywhere at any time, using the device that best fits the situation and task at hand (figure 24).

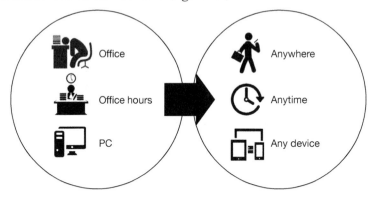

Figure 24: The shift from desktop working to mobile working

Research shows that employees of all age groups want more flexibility. They want flexibility to determine for themselves where, when, and how they work. Increased workplace flexibility has a positive effect on employee engagement and thereby on productivity.

A study by Virgin Media Business (2013) found that 40 percent of the surveyed organizations often overhear employees complaining they feel tied to their desks. Seven in ten organizations believed flexible working would make their employees both happier and more productive, boosting employee engagement.

Another study researched employee engagement within US governments. It found that while employee engagement is declining government-wide, satisfaction with working flexibility is rising and affecting employee engagement positively (U.S. Office of Personnel Management, 2013). Workplace flexibility *is* important to many employees. In a survey that AstraZeneca conducted among employees at their headquarter and R&D in Delaware, as many as 96 percent of the respondents answered that the flexibility offered influenced their decision to stay at AstraZeneca. 73 percent answered that it was 'very important' in that decision. Deloitte claim to have saved $41.5 million in employee turnover costs by retaining employees who, had they not offered workplace flexibility, would have left the company (Kossek, Hammer, Thompson & Burke, 2014).

What we are experiencing is a real paradigm shift. Physical proximity becomes less and less a prerequisite for working together. Most of the tasks that knowledge workers perform can be accomplished from any location, even those that require close collaboration with others. The enabling technologies are available. But adoption is lagging and a lot of employees don't know how to use these technologies effectively.

It is clearer than ever that presence does not equal productivity for knowledge work. So why aren't more organizations embracing workplace flexibility? One reason is the challenge it presents to managers. If they don't manage by results, then they manage by presence. And how do you do that when the subordinates are not at the office?

MEASURE THE OUTCOME INSTEAD OF THE TIME PUT IN

In the agricultural society, work used to be about what you could produce. The value created at a farm was measured by the quantity and quality of the harvest, not the amount of hours the people at the farm spent working out on the fields. Then we moved into factories and started measuring productivity by time spent at the factory.

The introduction of the time clock, invented in 1888 by jeweler Willard Bundy, reinforced the value of time and presence. It tracked the number of hours an employee worked and was the main measure by which work was judged and workers were paid. The more time the worker spends at the assembly line, the more output he or she would produce.

This is the way we have measured productivity of human resources since the start of the industrial revolution. Enchanted by the simplicity of this way to measure productivity, management has embraced and applied the same measure on practically all kinds of work. If the productivity per time unit could not easily be significantly increased, it is easy to add more man-hours to increase the productivity per employee.

Whether time spent at work is a relevant measure or not depends upon the nature of work we do. But for knowledge workers such as marketing and sales people, engineers, software developers, and creative professionals, it is an irrelevant productivity measure. Time spent at the office isn't the same thing as working or being productive. And putting in more hours doesn't have to increase productivity.

For knowledge workers, long hours often translate to decreased productivity and quality. People who work long hours show worse judgment and become less creative than those who don't. They are also more likely to suffer from anxiety, depression, or other health issues owing to a failing immune system (Surowiecki, 2014). Despite this, many *knowledge intensive* companies arc still managed on the assumption that investing more time will yield better results. Bob Pozen, senior lecturer at Harvard Business School, puts it like this:

> *"The real question is what you produce, not how many hours you put in. If you really are fast and can figure out a good solution quickly, you are in a sense penalized because you are not being able to bill as many hours... At one point in my youth, I was a lawyer billing hours and I would say that that really does create a perverse set of incentives"*

> *Pozen (2011)*

Pfeffer & Sutton (2000) attributes this to confusion between what is required to perform routine manual tasks well, and what is required to perform non-routine cognitive tasks:

> *"People in business, particularly men, often draw on analogies from physical competition such as various sports to guide their thinking about how work should be organized and rewarded... Hundreds of studies show that intellectual tasks that require learning and inventing new ways of doing things are best performed under drastically different conditions than tasks that have been done over and over again in the past.*

> *Pfeffer & Sutton (2000)*

WINNING WITH EMPLOYEE ENGAGEMENT

Falling engagement can likely be attributed to the lack of support and proper conditions for employees to do their jobs as well as they would like. New generations of employees, knowledge workers in particular, want more from their jobs than just a paycheck and job security. They have already learned that job security is an illusion in today's business environment.

Management in most organizations is blind to the waste of information work happening before their eyes, deaf to the cries from employees about stress and frustration, and apparently paralyzed in their ability to drive necessary changes. One explanation is that management is still acting on assumptions about productivity that originate from the 20th century. Back then, work was mostly manual, linear, predictable, and routine-based. Management could increase productivity by automating tasks and adding more man-hours, more structure, and more training.

As illustrated in figure 25, there is a gap between what many managers think drives knowledge worker productivity and what actually does.

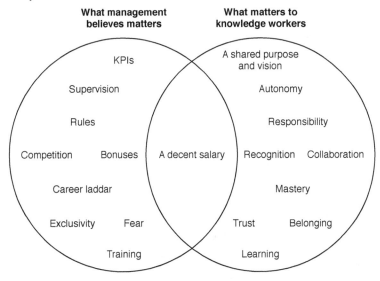

Figure 25: What makes knowledge workers productive

For example, many managers overemphasize training, but fail to consider and create the necessary conditions for enabling continuous and informal learning in the workplace. They believe monetary incentives like bonuses will motivate knowledge workers to be more productive. Yet most just want decent pay and be able to focus on their jobs without thinking about money.

Many of management's underlying assumptions about knowledge workers are wrong. You can see evidence of that in job ads. The Venn diagram above also serves to illustrate the gap between what job ads say versus what job shifters are seeking. So what are they looking for?

People looking for knowledge work typically want:

- a decent salary
- a clear and shared purpose, an articulated and engaging vision to strive for
- to be trusted and be given the responsibility and mandate that allows them to make decisions about things they know best
- a lean work situation, with as little unnecessary administration and waste as possible
- to be connected and take part in a thriving community where their knowledge, skill sets, and personality traits are being used to the fullest, and appreciated

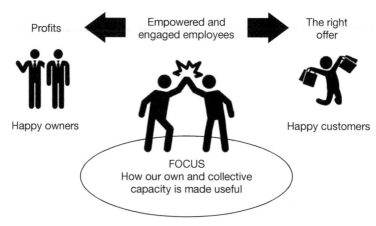

Figure 26: Empowered and engaged employees

Empowering people to do their jobs better and get the most out of their knowledge, skill sets, and personal traits will make them more engaged. We can learn from Lean philosophy in this respect. We should focus on the individuals and groups and give them the means to make sure they can create value. We should remove things that are wasteful or cause friction (figure 26). If we do, chances are people will become empowered and feel more engaged in their work.

CHAPTER 6

MAKING INFORMATION FLOW LIKE WATER

"All businesses are media businesses,
because whatever else they do,
all businesses rely on the managing of information for two audiences –
employees and the world." (Incsys, 2012)

Clay Shirky
Writer, consultant and teacher
on the social and economic effects of Internet technologies

The human body is, depending on sex and age, around 45 to 65 percent water. To function, we need to drink between one and two liters of water per day. Exactly how much we need depends on the situations we're in; what we do, the temperature, humidity, and several other factors.

Easy access to clean and fresh water is essential to survival and a prospering society. Since the dawn of history, humans have always settled close to freshwater watercourses or wetlands. Then, at some point, we learned how to dig wells to fetch water we could use for drinking, cooking, and cleaning. That gave us the option to settle across many more locations. But the water was not necessarily clean, and if someone dug a well in their backyard, they might not share their water with others. Fresh water was still a scarce resource and getting easy access to water meant everything for people and businesses. Later, as our cities grew and urban planning developed, we learned to plan and build public water supply systems that provided us with clean and fresh water. Water became a utility to those of us in the developed world, and we have learned to trust our water departments to provide uninterrupted clean water at a reasonable price.

As water is essential to human survival and a prospering society, so is information. When we communicate with each other, we exchange information that allows us to make decisions, as individuals or as a group. Lacking important information can be fatal.

Let's say you are out mushroom hunting and have little knowledge about wild mushrooms. Chances are you will end up with mushrooms that are deadly or dangerous for your health to consume in your basket. Yet you could easily reduce this risk. You could buy a book with instructions on how to identify and gather wild mushrooms. Or you could bring along a friend knowledgeable about mushrooms. In any case, you would get access to valuable information to help you pick the right mushrooms.

Continuing with the analogy between information and water, there are some additional similarities:

- Information, like water, needs to be accessible to us when and where they need it.
- Information, like water, needs to come from a source we trust if we are to use it.
- Information, like water, needs to be of sufficient quality to be suited for its intended uses.
- Information, like water, needs to flow to remain fresh and usable.
-

Regardless of where you are in a society, you should be able trust that the water is consistent, has met a certain a level of quality, and if you open the faucet, it will flow. It is the same with information. You need to access and trust the information you need. We can also capture information, and store it in on physical or digital media. Capturing information makes it easier to control both access to and the quality of the information. But we must always remember that information, like water, is a dynamic resource. It is constantly changing, and it needs to flow freely to remain fresh.

Making information flow between people is fundamental for collaboration and knowledge exchange to happen. It will help individuals, organizations and our society to survive and prosper. Just like water.

INFORMATION EXISTS ONLY IN OUR HEADS

Information is the lifeblood of an organization. If it was considered important before, it is even more important now that the business environment is becoming more and more dynamic, unpredictable, and competitive. To be competitive, an organization needs to ensure that it can access the right information fast, and turn it into action. Those that are able to do that have a comparative advantage to those that aren't.

Emerging technologies and concepts such as Big Data, advanced nalytics and artificial intelligence are all about that – collecting and analyzing huge amounts of data that is quickly turned into actionable information and insights.

When creating, keeping, and sharing information with each other, we have a variety of technologies to make use of. A couple of centuries ago we had only the written language, our first information technology. Since then we have invented many new and disruptive information technologies, such as the telegraph, the telephone, the calculator, and the computer (Gleick, 2011). Each of these innovations has changed our societies, businesses, and life in ways we couldn't predict or even imagine.

Harnessing the power of new information technology is a must today, and to properly design and use the technology one must understand what information is. So what is information? It might seem like a simple question to answer, but if you would ask someone what information is, most people would find it really hard to answer your question.

Generally, information is something that tells us something about a certain subject. It can be information that tells us if a certain mushroom is edible or not. It can tell us what a poisonous mushroom looks like, such as color and shape. Information results from a successful communication process: a message that has been sent from a sender and received, interpreted, and understood by a receiver (figure 27). The message can be transmitted directly using voice and body language. But it could also be transmitted indirectly via some artifact, such as text and images in a book or web page.

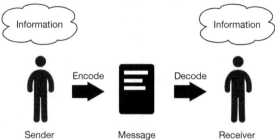

Figure 27: Information is transferred through a communication process

Despite what you might think, information is not something that exists in the physical or digital world. Information is something that is created in our heads, by cognitive processes in our brains. As a receiver of a transmitted message, you must already know something about the concepts that a message refers to to interpret and understand the message and extract information from it. If you don't have this pre-understanding, then the message will mean little or nothing to you. You won't be able to make sense out of it.

For example, if you don't know that much about the engineering of cars and how they work, then you probably won't understand what the sentence "your car's electronic fuel injection system is broken" means. If you have a pre-understanding about the concept of a car, you will understand that something is broken in your car. But if you lack pre-understanding of the concept of an 'electronic fuel injection system', you cannot understand what it broken. To understand, you will first have to find information that explains what the 'electronic fuel injection system' is and what it does.

The point is that we should not see information as an object. In the digital world, for example, everything we create, distribute, exchange, and consume is just some digital content intended to transmit information. This means, paradoxically, that we cannot manage the actual information with information technology, only the message.

To achieve effective communication, we need to create messages with the receiver in mind; anticipate the amount of pre-understanding the receiver has and adapt the message accordingly. Our ability to turn information into action requires that someone think really hard about who will need it, for what, and when before creating a message.

INFORMATION HAS NO VALUE IF IT IS NOT USED

If information is something that says something about a subject, then knowledge is our theoretical or practical understanding of a subject. One can say that knowledge comprises what we already know and that information comprises what we should know that we don't already.

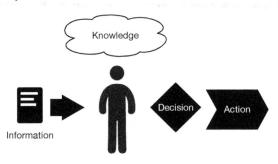

Figure 28: Information and knowledge fuel decisions and actions

Knowledge and information are the resources we use when performing tasks that aim to achieve a certain goal or satisfy a certain need or desire (see figure 28). When we receive a piece of information, the reason we might find it relevant and might keep it in our memory is often because we believe it might be useful to us. We believe it will help us achieve a goal or satisfy a need, either now or at some point in time. We cannot keep everything in our heads. If it isn't already written or captured as digital content, then we write or capture it and save it somewhere so we can find it when we have use for it later on.

It is one thing to find, capture, and save information that is relevant, and another thing to be able to use it. Information that might be of use holds a potential value to us, but that value is not realized until we use it for something. Information, and knowledge as well, is just a means to an end, and there is no value in information that is not being used at some point in time. Thus, to maximize the value of some information, the information needs to flow to the people who need it, whenever and wherever they need it. If it doesn't, its potential value will not be realized in full. We might invest a lot of time and effort into creating a report or graphic, but it is only when someone is able to access, interpret, understand and act on it that the investment we have made pays off. The more people that can access it and find a good use for it, the more value it will create.

INFORMATION WANTS TO BE FREE

The first Hackers' Conference took place at an old army base in Marin County, California, in the fall of 1984. During the conference, Stewart Brand, who arranged the conference together with Kevin Kelly and at the time was editor of the Whole Earth Catalog, made the following remark in a reply to something Apple's co-founder Steve Wozniak said:

> "On the one hand information wants to be expensive, because it's so valuable. The right information in the right place just changes your life. On the other hand, information wants to be free, because the cost of getting it out is getting lower and lower all the time. So you have these two fighting against each other."

> Brand, Kelly & Dyson (2011)

Later, in 1985, Kevin Kelly published the remark in the CoEvolution Quarterly. The phrase "information wants to be free" soon became a catchphrase for hackers and part of hacker ethics, and turned into a religion to some, as it was used in the fight against the forces that wanted to limit the access to information.

Richard Stallman, an American software freedom activist and the founder of the Free Software Foundation who has been known to be an advocate for the idea of making all information free, argued that all generally useful information should be free in the sense that anyone can copy and adapt it to one's own uses (Denning, 1990).

No matter what position one might take in the conflict between those who want all information to be freely available and those who fight to protect ownership and intellectual property rights, it should be obvious that the same kind of conflict does not exist for information inside an organization. From a purely rational point of view, you would want all employees to make the best possible decisions – decisions that contribute to the shared purpose and greater good of the organization.

To be able to do this, an employee needs to be able to understand the full context and have access to all information that is available and relevant when making a decision. If you want people in an organization to align and push things in the same direction, then you must ensure that they all have access to the same information. Unless it is absolutely necessary, you would want to avoid information asymmetry, a situation where someone has more or better information than the others ("Information asymmetry", 2015). Any occurrence of information asymmetry within an organization should be a rare exception. However, in most organizations information asymmetry is very common. It can be the result of politics or lack of incentives or technical ability to share and make information easily accessible across the organization. Ultimately, these can all be seen as symptoms of a lack of understanding of the value free-flowing information can create.

There are many reasons why information should be allowed to flow freely within an organization. Take innovation as an example. You never know when or where innovation will happen, where ideas will pop up and where they will come to life. But if information does not flow freely, innovation is less likely to happen. Ideas simply need to be allowed to find the place where they have the right conditions to shoot off and grow. Information is the carrier of ideas, and communication is about moving information (ideas) from one place (mind) to another.

Organizations often safeguard information in ways that restrict, block, or completely obfuscate it from employees who need it. There are reasons for this irrational behavior. According to James Boyle, chairman of Creative Commons and teacher of law at Duke, one such reason is that we don't understand the benefits of openness. We overestimate the benefits of closed systems. Boyle argues that humans are risk averse and have a systematic bias against openness. We don't expect collaboration and openness to bring the kind of benefits they do. To illustrate this, Boyle used the example of Wikipedia:

> "…in 1990 you are asked to assemble the greatest encyclopedia, in most languages, updated in real time, adopt a neutral point of view. In 1990, you'd say that you need maybe a billion dollars, a hierarchical corporation, lots of editors, vet the writers you're hiring, peer reviewers, copyright it all to recoup the money we've invested, trademark it. And someone else says, 'We'll have a web site, and people will like put stuff up and people will edit it.' How many of us would have picked #2? We don't understand openness."
>
> Weinberger (2008)

Perhaps we would behave differently if we could see and acknowledge the risks that are associated with *not* being open and sharing freely. In organizations, these risks manifest themselves as bad decision-making, sub-optimization, rework, and low levels of reuse. Lack of openness and transparency leads to trust failure, making people share and collaborate less. As a result organizations become less productive, less innovative, and less capable of adapting to changing conditions.

Although it needs to be easy to restrict access to information when necessary, openness should be the default and secrecy the exception. Protecting something from others within the same organization should require a motivated decision and an active effort to set the proper protection level. If something is worth

protecting, it should also be worth the effort of protecting it.
We shouldn't start with blaming people for not sharing until we
have made sharing the default option in our systems, be it our
personal calendars or information created and used within a team.
If openness isn't the default stance, chances are people see it as
optional and won't do it unless they need to and can see a clear
'what's in it for me'.

If sharing is hard to do, people will be less inclined to share.
When they really need to share something they will often try to
find more convenient and less secure ways to do so. Some people
share information by saving it on USB sticks that might get lost or
become vehicles for spreading computer viruses from one device to
another. Other people decide to use commercial file sharing services
or even via their private online email accounts. To avoid this, ease of
use and security must be properly balanced.

THE DARK MATTER OF THE INFORMATION UNIVERSE

Organizations create and capture huge amounts of data and
information, most of which relate to transactions and business
processes. But how much does the typical organization know
about the conversations taking place between people within the
organization?

Truth is most business conversations are transient and leave
few traces. Typically, only the individuals that participate in the
conversation know that it ever took place and what it was about.
This is because the vast majority of business conversations either
take place over phone, face-to-face, or in closed channels such as
email. When conversations are buried in email inboxes they are
almost impossible to access for anyone who didn't take part in the
conversation. In a way, most business conversations are like dark
matter. We know it must be there, but we can't observe it and don't
know what it actually consists of.

As organizations become more reliant on rapid access to the
right information, this becomes a great problem. If the Customer

Service or Support department is outsourced, it becomes harder to transfer the information they capture and the knowledge they build about customer behaviors and needs to the Research and Development (R&D) department. If production processes are outsourced to one or several partners, it becomes harder for R&D to learn about what works in production and what doesn't. And the Sales and Marketing department have even less control over when to execute activities.

This challenge clearly hasn't gotten enough attention, and organizations need to make much bigger efforts to ensure relevant information is made explicit, findable, and accessible to those who need it, whenever and wherever they need it.

THERE IS A LONG TAIL OF INFORMATION NEEDS

In a rapidly changing and uncertain business environment, it is often very hard or even impossible to anticipate what information is needed, by whom and when. The information might not even exist until the moment it is needed, or you might be unaware of its existence in the first place. That's why 'more is better' when it comes to information supply in such a business environment. If there is more information to choose from, chances are there will be something for (almost) any need that arises. That is why it has become critical for knowledge workers to have access to the abundance of information on the Internet. They also need to have immediate access to anyone who might possess the knowledge and information they need.

Organizations typically try to serve their employees' information needs by identifying typical needs and producing information to serve these needs. Owing to limited resources, not all information needs can be served. The line needs to be drawn somewhere, and it is usually drawn where the cost of providing a certain piece of information exceeds the potential value of the information.

The easiest way to estimate the value of a certain piece of information is to measure its usage rate. Usage rate is a measure of the demand for a piece of information per unit of time, such as a week or month. It is interesting to look at how frequently it is being used, but also at how many people use it. If someone frequently uses a certain piece of information, we can assume the information is valuable to him or her. If a lot of people use the same piece of information, it is valuable to a lot of people.

This way of measuring the value of information is a bit blunt and can sometimes be misleading for example when there is information that is supposed to never be used but yet is absolutely critical to provide access to. One such example is the aforementioned Standard Operating Procedures for emergency situations in a power plant. Furthermore, measuring information value this way becomes dysfunctional when it is necessary to meet information needs that cannot easily be anticipated, and when the need is different from time to time. Although a piece of information might only be used once it might still have tremendous value. Let us use the long tail power graph in figure 29, to illustrate this reasoning.

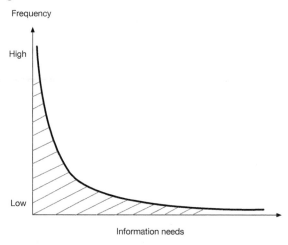

Figure 29: Long tail power graph of information needs

The most frequent information needs are located in the left end of the power graph, the neck. In the tail we find less frequent information needs. If the majority of the information needs belong to this group, the power graph is said to have a long tail. This is likely the case for knowledge-intense organizations, especially those that operate in rapidly changing and uncertain business environments. This means that such an organization cannot simply neglect to serve the needs in the long tail.

THE COST OF SERVING INFORMATION NEEDS

What is the cost of serving an information need? A simple way to estimate this cost is to define it as the aggregated cost of producing, distributing, and managing the information resource that is intended to serve the information need. We can call this the 'cost to serve' (see figure 30).

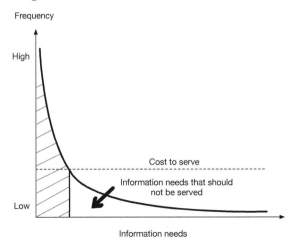

Figure 30: High cost to serve means a lot of information needs don't get served

The lower the cost to serve is, the more information needs can be served. As a general rule of thumb, an information need should be served if the value of the information is greater than the cost of producing, distributing, and managing it. Assuming an organization relies on the usage rate as the primary measure of what information is valuable and needed, then it will conclude that it should focus on serving common information needs. It will strive to serve the information needs in the neck of the power graph.

If the cost of producing, distributing, and managing the required information is equal to or greater than the value of the information, then the information need should not be served. If the information already exists, the organization might even choose to delete it so that it does not get in the way of more valuable information that people need. Following this reasoning, an organization should focus on producing, distributing, and managing information where the value of the information measured as usage rate exceeds the cost to serve.

THE GAME PLAN HAS CHANGED

The technological developments during recent years have provided less tech-savvy users with affordable and easy-to-use tools and devices that allow them to create and share information with other people across the globe at almost no cost. Using the Internet as a platform, people collaborate to create, distribute and manage information.

This has completely changed the game plan when it comes to serving information needs within organizations. The resources an organization can employ to create, distribute, and manage information resources are no longer limited to a handful of people. Moreover, it can be done at a fraction of the cost and time that used to be needed. The cost to serve has fallen dramatically. Organizations now have a great opportunity to serve the long tail of information needs that become increasingly important to serve.

If we take a look at the long tail power graph again (figure 31), the information needs in the long neck are likely to arise from routine work. This kind of work does not change very often. The same information is needed over and over again. The information needs are repeatable and predictable. An information need that has arisen once will, for certain, do so again. This allows us to define, design, and produce information that will serve those needs in advance.'

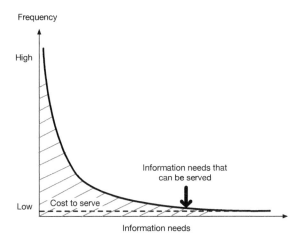

Figure 31: The cost to serve information needs has collapsed

THE LONG TAIL OF INFORMATION NEEDS MUST BE SERVED

For non-routine knowledge work, on the other hand, most of the information needs are likely to be found in the long tail. The information need varies from time to time, from situation to situation. A piece of information might be used a few times, or maybe even only once, by a few people, or maybe by a single individual. This makes it more or less impossible to define a reusable information resource before it is actually needed, or to know the value it will have to the person who needs it. Seemingly trivial information might have immense value.

Under these conditions, trying to decide beforehand what information should be made accessible to users and what shouldn't is a bad strategy. Since it is impossible to anticipate all information that might be needed, or what value it will have, an organization cannot put the relevant information in one 'for keeps' pile, and all other information in another 'to be trashed' pile. Instead, it needs to ensure that as much information as possible can be captured and made accessible to those who might need it.

CHAPTER 7

AVOIDING INFORMATION OVERLOAD

*"Findability precedes usability.
In the alphabet and on the Web.
You can't use what you can't find."*

*Peter Morville
Pioneer of the fields of information architecture and user experience*

Literacy didn't become a concern in the western world until the 19th century and most of the books were kept in monasteries, universities, and private homes rather than in public libraries; so few people could read the books, much less search for information in the books.

When put in perspective against the whole of human history, the behavior of actively searching for information is brand new. During the past two centuries, we have captured so much information we have been forced to develop sophisticated and complex methods to find and access the information (Bates, 2003). Not only is the behavior of actively searching for information new to humans, but it is also the opposite of how we have acquired information throughout human history. Most of the information we receive comes from passively observing people and events in our environment.

As Marcia J. Bates writes in her research paper from 2003, "it is not unreasonable to guess that we absorb perhaps 80 percent of all our knowledge through simply being aware, being conscious and sentient in our social context and physical environment".

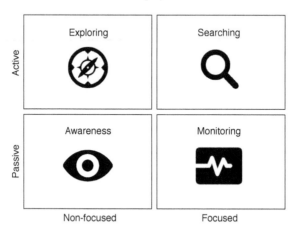

Figure 32: Classification of information seeking methods

If not lazy, humans are economical by nature. The *principle of least effort* tells us that people will use the most convenient method to achieve a certain outcome, and that we are satisfied as soon as the results are acceptable ("Principle of least effort", 2015). We don't like to waste our time and resources.

Therefore, we are likely to use the method that requires the least effort when we look for information. We even use less reliable information if it's just easy to find and use. If the information we need is accessible and easy to consume we would rather use that information than to actively search for more robust alternatives somewhere else. Searching just doesn't come naturally to us.

The natural way for humans to learn something is through observation, passively receiving and reacting to information in our environment. A lot of interpretations are done by processes in our subconsciousness. We react to things happening in our environment. We often call this *intuition*: we have learned how something in our environment works, and when it happens we make immediate decisions without being able to explain afterwards how we arrived at the decision. When we do something by intuition, it doesn't mean that our brains aren't active or don't interpret information. It's just that it happens "automatically" in our subconsciousness. For example, an experienced driver develops an intuitive sense of what to expect on the road and can react in the right way instantaneously when a situation arises.

So it isn't all that surprising that most people invest as little effort as possible in searching for information and developing the required skills to do so. It is mostly when we have a specific and urgent need or interest that we spontaneously try to develop our information seeking skills.

NOT FINDING INFORMATION IS COSTLY

Information is a key asset when running an enterprise today. An enterprise that gets access to the right information at the right time and is able turn it into actionable knowledge before anyone else has a comparative advantage.

Despite this common sense, there is plenty of research that points out that information isn't considered as important as it should be by organizations. There is often a gap between knowing it is important and doing something about it that results in poor information management.

A study by The Data Warehousing Institute (2002) estimated that poor information quality costs organizations 10-20 percent of operating revenue in process failure and 'information scrap and rework' in direct costs. What is even more interesting is that although 83 percent of the participating companies in the study thought they had a lot of information of bad quality, 80 percent thought the cost for bad information quality was below 0.1 percent of revenue.

Research by the Association for Information and Image Management, AIIM, tells us that 52 percent of organizations have 'little or no confidence' that their digital information is 'accurate, accessible, and trustworthy' (Mancini, 2008). Yet, over 90 percent of organizations view their ability to manage electronic information as critical to their future.

Even for organizations that claim to understand how great the negative impact of bad information quality really is, the sheer size of the challenge might scare them from tackling it. Cutting costs in transactional processes is just so much easier to do. In 2001, Feldman and Sherman (2001) found that the average knowledge worker spent 15 percent to 35 percent of their workday searching for information. Fifteen percent of the time was spent duplicating existing information. Searching for information is successful around half of the time. Even though more than a decade has passed since their findings were published, not much suggests the situation has improved, especially since the amount of information created by organizations is often said to be increasing almost exponentially.

Although the costs of not being able to find and access information fast enough are often high, the costs of not being able to find a certain piece of information at all is potentially even higher, resulting in rework, delays, unresponsive customer service, bad decision making... you name it. All of these things happen frequently due to the lack of access to the right information at the right time – and often the information isn't accessible in the first place. Or as Feldman expressed it:

> *"While the costs of not finding information are enormous, they are hidden within the enterprise, and therefore they are rarely perceived as having an impact on the bottom line. Decisions are usually information problems. If they are made with poor or erroneous information, then they put the life of the enterprise at stake. Therefore, it behooves the enterprise to provide the best information-finding tools available and to ensure that all of its intellectual assets have access to them, no matter where they reside."*

Findability is, according to Peter Morville (2005), "the ability to find anyone or anything from anywhere at anytime". It is important to understand that we are looking for concepts, not terms. Findability has a major impact on workforce productivity, innovation, and quality. It can mean the difference between success and failure on the individual level as well as on the organizational and enterprise level.

There are multiple seeking strategies; some are more natural and economical to humans than search, and thus search needs to be complemented with additional solutions to serve the rising demand for information in an organization or enterprise. This requires ensuring that the content carrying information is accessible and described in the right way, so it can be found in the right contexts and presented to the user in a smart way, supporting discovery. Since relevance is relative to who is looking for information, the information about the user, task, and context need to be considered when presenting information to the user.

DRINKING FROM THE INFORMATION FIRE HOSE

"23 Exabytes of information was recorded and replicated in 2002. We now (2011) record and transfer that much information every 7 days."

Finley (2011)

Information glut, data smog, drinking from the information fire hose, drowning in a sea of information, and information overload. Same thing, different words. What they all say is that we are provided with more information than we can process and absorb. Information overload, a term popularized by Alvin Toffler in his bestseller 'Future Shock' from 1970, occurs then a system receives more input than it has capacity to process.

If we had unlimited cognitive capacity, then it wouldn't be a problem to receive, make sense of, and remember everything we see, hear, or feel. But, as we all intuitively know from our own experiences, our capacity to receive, interpret, and keep information is very limited. When we receive more information than we can handle, it becomes harder for us to make decisions, and we experience stress.

The amount of digital information we create increases almost exponentially, or at least it multiplies by ten every five years. This trend, sometimes described as an information tsunami or information explosion, is often blamed for causing information overload; there is just too much information. It is hard to argue against the idea that the volume of information is related to information overload, but that doesn't mean that the solution to overload must be to remove information, or to stop people from sharing more information. Our production of new information has turned into a force of nature, something we can no longer control or stop, at least not without sacrificing the progress of our society. Unless we want to radically alter our information production, and risk hampering societal progress, we need to accept and adjust to this time of information abundance. We will continue to create more and more information, and we must find other solutions for dealing with it.

In the introduction chapter of Thomas Allen's famous book 'Managing the Flow of Technology' from 1977, Allen writes about the information explosion and how the tremendous increase in information presents a problem to scientists, as they have to slog through "a morass of available information to reach the information pertinent to his problem." He also suggests that we need to design systems to serve the user, ensuring that they suit their needs, habits, and preferences. Not much has changed since then. We still have the same concerns, we still create more and more information, and we are still creating solutions that help us deal with the information explosion.

Clay Shirky (2008) argues that the term 'information overload' is being overutilized. It is used to dismiss many of the questions we need to ask ourselves in the information society; it is an excuse to avoid looking for and learning new solutions for dealing with large volumes of information. If there is a problem with the amount of information being created, it is not the amount of information *per se*, but rather the amount of duplicated, incorrect, and irrelevant information that is not traceable to any creator or owner and therefore cannot be trusted even if it – against all odds – is found. A key part in a solution is to make existing information visible, accessible, and possible to reuse without copying it.

THE QUEST FOR BETTER FILTERS

Try to imagine walking into the Royal Library of Alexandria in Egypt a decade before Christ. The library, which was likely destroyed in a fire set by Julius Caesar in 48 BC, was to collect all the world's knowledge. It has been estimated to have contained hundreds of thousands of papyrus scrolls. When walking into the library, it is likely that you would be overwhelmed, with no clue as how to navigate the vast assortment of records.

Although we know little about the library today, there had to be a system for organizing the scrolls and tools such as indexes for navigating that system, much like in a modern library. To find the desired information, you would either have to learn to understand the organization system and how to use the tools to navigate it, or ask a librarian or more experienced scholar for help. In the digital age we no longer have a limited number of shelves and physical space to put the books on or the high cost of producing, distributing, and managing books (or scrolls). The Internet has become our shared global library, giving us access to an abundance of information.

Even though the vast majority of information on the Internet is of little or no interest to you, each piece of information is likely to interest at least someone in the world. Rather than limiting the amount of information on the Internet and stopping people from publishing their works, we should focus on improving on the organization systems and provide better navigation tools. Similarly, when people complain about over-flooded inboxes at work, the solution should not be to limit the amount of information that is created and made accessible to them. Instead we should create better tools and solutions for sharing and finding relevant information.

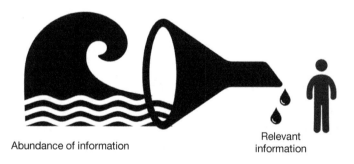

Abundance of information

Relevant information

Figure 33: We need better filters

Clay Shirky (2008) puts it this way:

> *"Instead of blaming the abundance of information available*
> *in the connected age, it's consumers' duty to continue*
> *to evolve with the systems – and to reconfigure their*
> *information filters, both culturally and technologically...*
> *When you feel yourself getting too much information, it's not*
> *to say to yourself 'What's happened to the information?' It's*
> *to say, 'What filter just broke?'"*

As humans we are reliant on our senses and cognitive processes in our brains to help us filter out the tiny bits of information relevant to us from the enormous amounts of information we are exposed to everyday of our lives. People diagnosed with autism have sensory difficulties that make it hard for them to focus their attention on important information and filtering out background information. Recent research points to people with autism lacking a "social hormone" called oxytocin that promotes social bonding and helps information and sensory processing from the senses through the brain. One can say we need to develop the digital equivalent of this social hormone.

METADATA FOR THE PEOPLE, BY THE PEOPLE

David Weinberger is often quoted for having said that "the cure to information overload is more information". At first glance, this statement might seem provoking: can we really deal with the increasing volumes of information by creating *more* information? Yes, we can, as long as it is metadata.

Metadata is information about information. It tells you something essential about the book, document, or video you are looking for, such as what it is called, who authored it, and where you can find it. Metadata is the information you would find on an index card in a library. Its purpose is to answer specific questions we have about the information we are looking for, such as where it can be found or how we may use it.

Metadata can be either explicit or implicit. Implicit metadata is created automatically by a digital solution and hence does not require any human intervention. It is derived when the user does something, such watching a video on Youtube. If the user likes the video or adds it to a list of favourites, then explicit metadata is created. That is, the user creates an immediately identifiable piece of metadata. The latter is also what is called user-generated metadata - it has been created by end users of a piece of content. Metadata that is created by the person or organization that produced the video is called producer-generated. Some examples of these different types of metadata are listed in figure 34.

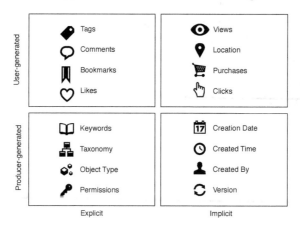

Figure 34: Examples of different types of metadata

For a long time, in the personal computing era, metadata was more or less synonymous with file properties; file name, location, date created, and so forth. This metadata was hidden and hence remained unknown to most users. It was mostly of technical character, which made it hard to understand for regular users. It did not really help people. In an age of information abundance, this had to change.

As Voltaire said, perfect is the enemy of good. The ambition with metadata should not be to create perfect metadata, but rather to create useful and usable metadata. Users should not need to spend time and energy on trying to understand detailed metadata or weird terms with complex syntax. The metadata must be easy to read, interpret, and understand.

To create useful metadata, you need to have knowledge about both the content and its intended uses. There is also often a need to create different metadata for the same content since the same metadata might not be usable for all intended uses and users. That is why the task of creating metadata traditionally has been assigned to 'metadata professionals' such as librarians.

Recently, however, creating metadata has become something 'ordinary' people can do. Even if the metadata is not perfect in the eyes of the expert, it might serve the purpose just as good or better than the metadata that the expert would come up with. It's metadata for the people, by the people.

CHAPTER 8

ESCAPING
THE TYRANNY
OF EMAIL

"Email is where knowledge goes to die."

Bill French

Until recently, most efforts aimed at improving information work and workforce collaboration focused on making individual workers or teams perform better. Organizations have created digital work environments to optimize personal productivity and teamwork, but in doing so they have neglected that information work is increasingly reliant upon collaboration in networks across locations and organizations – stretching far beyond teams.

It might seem a paradox, but our digital work environments have in fact made us more isolated and unaware of what is happening at work. It was easier to be involved back when we were physically closer to the people we worked with. Nowadays, knowledge workers need to interact with lots of people in different organizations and locations on a daily basis. Our digital work environments don't provide the transparency and openness that is required if we are to see what is happening elsewhere. This makes it hard to make contributions that benefit the company as a whole, such as sharing information with people outside our own teams. This is something that creates inefficiencies, duplicate work, sub-optimization, lost innovations, low reuse of knowledge and solutions, and so forth.

At the same time the complexity of our digital work environments is increasing. New tools and features are often deployed without taking the existing portfolio into consideration, and the usability of those tools are often poor. This is the consequence of technology-focus; failing to consider the needs and situations of the users. A study by Oracle (2012) supports this reasoning. The study showed that user-focused organizations are much more productive and profitable than technology-focused organizations. The productivity loss of tech-focused organizations was 2.3 times greater than user-focused organizations. User-focused organizations outperformed the tech-focused companies, achieving 23 percent higher revenue-per-employee against their industry peers. The study also found that the effective usage rates of enterprise software are down compared to two years ago, with users experiencing productivity losses of around 17 percent, translating to almost one day per week.

Despite the increasing complexity of our digital work environments, many knowledge workers still lack such basics as a complete set of good quality tools to do their jobs. The tools we have are often not designed for the work we need to do, and they are neither easy to use nor integrated in a way that makes work flow smoothly.

This not only hampers our productivity, but it is draining employee engagement. We are expected to perform better as management imposes new tools on us, but these tools have often been selected and designed without a proper understanding of the nature of our work, our needs and preferences, and the situations we work in.

We need a new and better approach for boosting knowledge worker productivity with digital technologies. This approach must, by necessity, take a holistic view on our digital work environment so that unnecessary complexity can be reduced or eliminated, and so knowledge workers are provided the right tools designed in the right way. We must also fill the technology gap that makes it hard to collaborate on highly interdependent and non-routine knowledge work. And we must change how we use existing technology, such as email.

THE TECHNOLOGY GAP

In situations when we need to communicate and collaborate with each other but are apart from each other in time and space, we need various communication technologies. This is a common scenario in large organizations. Yet, the support we have at hand is often not sufficient.

The heavy use of email is a symptom of this. Even though email is easy to use by the sender and can be used for virtually any purpose, it is ill-suited for collaboration and it seriously limits an organization's ability to make information available to all those who need it.

Figure 35: Legacy communication tools still dominate in most organizations

The vast majority of organizations continue to use traditional communication tools such as phone calls, emails, and face-to-face meetings to communicate and collaborate (figure 35). Although collaboration is an increasingly important activity to knowledge workers, we favor established and familiar collaborative tools over newer alternatives. We often rely on email and sending documents back and forth, which can lead to complaints about information overload due to full inboxes. Much of it is due to occupational spam, unwanted or unnecessary emails.

Current communication tools are also skewed towards broadcasting and push. This means that there is a need for new tools that can replace the use of email for collaboration. There is also a need for new tools that support highly interdependent non-routine work as illustrated in figure 36.

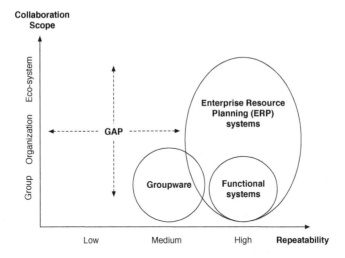

Figure 36: The technology gap in non-routine collaborative knowledge work

The tools organizations have introduced during the last couple of decades to support knowledge work – such as workflow systems, enterprise portals, intranets, and groupware – aren't good enough at supporting the fluid and unpredictable nature of non-routine knowledge work.

Workflow systems were introduced to support the execution of easily repeatable processes. Typical applications are product information management and content management processes where both the output and the structure of the processes can be defined in advance and are repeatable. Most workflow systems have usually been designed top-down and might not fit users' work-styles or integrate well with the rest of the components in a user's digital work environment. This often means that infrequent users try to avoid using these systems. The complexity of these systems creates a barrier to entry, requiring extensive training and education to use them in efficient and effective ways.

Groupware, or collaboration software as it is more often called today, is intended to support teamwork in virtual teams. Such collaboration software typically supports planning, coordination, communication, and sharing of information resources within a team, revolving around some digital workspace. But not all non-routine work is bound to a team or group, and not all types of collaborative work make the effort of setting up and maintaining a group workspace worthwhile. These tools are put in use when a team has already been formed, and they often fail to provide mechanisms that make information flow across teams and allow contributions from people outside the team.

To fill the gap left by workflow systems and groupware, many organizations have invested substantial time and resources in developing enterprise portals. The purpose of portals is to provide employees with single-point access to information from various sources and systems through a web-based user interface. The general design approach has been to segment the tasks and information needs of employees into different roles and to map a pre-defined set of tools and information sources to those roles.

Unfortunately, few enterprise portal initiatives have started out with an ambition to understand the characteristics of knowledge work, how it gets done, and how it can be done in a better way. They especially fail to address the needs of non-routine and highly collaborative knowledge work. Typical symptoms are low adoption and usage rates and the absence of any positive effects on knowledge worker productivity. Instead, employees revert to email to get their jobs done.

Then we have the intranet. Traditionally, the intranet has been a place for communicating corporate news to employees and giving them access to information about the organization, its processes and systems, as well as information that aims to help people perform routine tasks. A central editorial team usually manages the information on the intranet, being responsible for organizing the information and supervising the publishing of new information on the intranet. The right to publish information on the intranet might very well be decentralized to organizational groups so they can publish their own information, but it still doesn't make the intranet a natural place for employee-to-employee information sharing.

A lot of the information that employees need to share with each other would not have a natural place on the intranet and thus wouldn't fit in the centrally governed organization scheme. Besides, it is impossible for a central team to manage all the information that would end up on the intranet. They would need to draw the line somewhere and decline to publish some information on the intranet. Yet, the only ones who can determine whether a piece of information is relevant or not are the people that will eventually use it.

All of these solutions fall short in some way or another when it comes to supporting collaborative non-routine knowledge work. But why worry? We always have email.

EMAIL IS THE BIGGEST PRODUCTIVITY DRAIN

Multiple studies indicate that the average corporate employee spends around 25-30 percent of their workday on email related tasks. By comparison, we spend 14 percent of our time, or just 6.4 hours per week, on communicating and collaborating internally (McKinsey, 2012). This wouldn't be an issue if we were getting work done during all that time, but the fact is that a large portion of that time is spent simply on managing — organizing, archiving, deleting — the emails that we receive.

In addition, many of the emails we receive have nothing to do with work. According to a study by Mimecast (2012), around 7 percent of the emails we receive at work are spam or junk mail, and another 11 percent is personal or non-work-related; 63 percent of the emails are used for employee-to-employee communication.

Spending 25 to 30 percent of your workday on email-related tasks perhaps wouldn't be such a big problem if you did it all in one chunk, say during the first two hours of your day. Although you may be an exception that's not how most people manage their emails. That's not how email works.

Most people have their email application open, or at least have an app that notifies them about new mails. You get an email when the sender decides to send it to you, whether you want it or not, and whether it suits your work to read it or not. With email, anyone who has access to your email address can point and shoot whatever message they want at you. Potentially anything can end up in your inbox. Ubiquitous access to the most versatile communication tool makes it very easy to bombard people with information. And this bombardment goes on, continuously interrupting you from completing the task at hand.

It is commonly said that the average worker typically gets interrupted every seven or eight minutes. After each interruption it takes some time to return to the task that was disrupted, especially when it comes to serious mental tasks, such as programming or writing. When you have been interrupted you typically wander off to reply to other messages or browse the web. It is likely that you lose about two hours per day on interruptions and the time needed to refocus (Spira, 2009). That doesn't leave much time for being productive, does it?

Email is the biggest productivity drain for knowledge workers because it puts such a heavy burden on the recipient. It is up to the receiver, not the sender, to add structure to the communication and deal with the chaos in their inbox. All sorts of emails end up in our inboxes with no good way to identify or add context, or easily filter out what is irrelevant. It is entirely up to us as receivers to create filters and apply structure to the communication – and this has to be done by every individual who is participating in an email conversation, for all email conversations we participate in!

If we combine this with the phenomena of occupational spam, where there is no way for the recipient to opt out of some conversations they have been added to by the sender, the situation easily becomes unmanageable to many people and creates enormous amounts of waste in organizations.

EMAIL GETS MESSY WHEN COLLABORATING

Despite the introduction of communication tools such as instant messaging and video conferencing, most organizations still rely on email as their main means of communication. Physical meetings and phone calls are used in situations where email simply cannot be used.

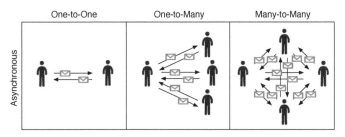

Figure 37: E-mail becomes messy as soon as the number of participants and amount of interaction grows

Looking at different types of communication, email has become the primary tool for all of them. If we look where email is used in the communication matrix model below (figure 37), it is easy to see that email-based communication becomes messy when more than two people are involved in a conversation.

Email becomes highly problematic in many-to-many interactions. If you try to have a conversation with just a few people over email, it easily gets out of hand. When we attach documents and use email for collecting feedback or creating content together, it gets even worse. Now not only the content of the email is duplicated for each email that is sent, but the attachments are as well. Keeping track of who changed what in the document and which file is the current version, or integrating changes into one single document when people have worked on individual copies, is time-consuming and sometimes seemingly impossible.

When email was first introduced in the late 1970s and early 1980s, work wasn't at all as collaborative, or geographically distributed, as it is today. The type of communication that took place between managers and employees was mostly one-way; early email use was not often 'many-to-many'. In other words, the amount and complexity of many-to-many conversations was very limited compared to today when there's so much communication happening between employees across time and space.

Still, when features such as 'reply all' and email lists were introduced in corporate email systems, the software engineers responsible knew what it would eventually lead to. They were well aware that email wasn't at all suitable for many-to-many communication; it would create a tsunami of information, causing information overload among information workers, and create oceans of duplicated information that would need to be managed. That's why they considered leaving features such as email lists out, but at some point, management made a demand, and, *ta-da*, email lists were introduced. 'Reply all' as well. Looking back, it was like opening Pandora's box.

NINE REASONS FOR EMAIL'S POPULARITY

To effectively fight the habit of email and replace it with better tools, one must first understand what makes it such a powerful and attractive tool. When you think about it, it isn't hard at all to see what characteristics have made email become so popular.

- **Versatile.** Email is a very versatile communication tool. We can use it to communicate about anything, for whatever purpose we might have.
- **Boundless**. Email overcomes the boundaries of time and space. We can get in contact and communicate with people from all over the world.

- **Universal reach.** Almost everybody has an email address. Even though it might be hard to find a person's address, we can can be almost certain they have one.

- **Asynchronous.** Unlike a phone call, email doesn't require the receiver to be present in order for the sender to start communicating.

- **Easy of use.** If you can read and write, and have basic computing skills, you can write an email. Enter the recipient's email address, type your message, and click 'send'.

- **Broadcasting.** You can reach as many people as you have email addresses. If you hit the limit of the number of emails you can put on the recipients list, usually around 1000, you can create an email list instead and put the list name as the recipient instead.

- **Ubiquitous access.** We can write and read our emails from almost anywhere as long as we have access to a computing device with a web browser or email client and an Internet connection.

- **Freeform.** Email doesn't pre-impose any specific structure to the message, other than it should have a subject that informs the recipient what the email is about. The sender is free to write and structure the message.

- **Social.** Email can help us get in contact with people, keep in touch with friends and colleagues, and initiate and maintain new relationships. We can interact and engage in conversations with other people on equal terms.

All of these characteristics go hand in hand with the nature of non-routine knowledge work. If we can assign these characteristics to new communication tools that compensate for the weaknesses of email, there is a good chance people will adopt these new tools and limit their email use to what it is best suited for – private one-to-one conversations.

BREAKING HABITS IS HARD

Despite the apparent advantages of email to regular mail, it took many years for people and organizations to make the shift. Now that it has been widely adopted and become the *de facto* standard for all kinds of communication inside and outside organizations, the amount of problems due to email overuse and misuse are piling up. Organizations have become dependent and addicted to email.

Over the years, given its convenient, ubiquitous, and freeform nature, email has developed some kind of monopoly over employee-to-employee communication. Emailing has become a habit. We use email without reflecting on how we use it. We don't ask ourselves if there are better ways to do some or all of the things we use email for. It is perfectly natural for us to use email for many-to-many conversations and for coordinating highly collaborative tasks. The fact that email is, by design, especially ill-suited for this doesn't stop us. Even though we feel overloaded with information and stressed out at work because of email, we aren't willing to let it go. Our brains are now wired for email.

The overuse of email is not only a problem for individuals, but also a great problem for organizations where efficient communication, collaboration, and knowledge exchange is essential. We all know that habits are hard to change and changing habits is a great challenge for organizations. They need to constantly question and change old habits; and one of the habits they need to question and change is how they use email.

Looking a bit broader, organizations need to reflect on current attitudes and behaviors, and identify opportunities for improvement regarding how people communicate, share information, and collaborate with each other. Speaking in terms of technology, they need to look beyond traditional and well-established tools and technologies such as email, and evaluate how other tools and technologies can support more efficient communication, collaboration, and knowledge exchange.

A lot of employees are aware of the problems with internal email, or at least the symptoms such as information overload and the inability to find information shared via email. But not much is being done about it.

A likely reason for the lack of change is that email has been seen as a perfect tool for managers to communicate with their subordinates, leaving little room for feedback loops, dialogue and open discussions among the employees. It feels safer that no one outside the list of the recipients can see what they are communicating and to whom. Why expose yourself to the risk of some external stakeholder questioning what is being communicated, or asking for more information? This has fostered a culture that is the opposite of the one we associate with external social media. Over the years, email has become an institution for management communication. It is perhaps a bit naive to expect the people who created the institution and are dependent on its existence will destroy it. Only visionaries and leaders will be able to do it.

CHAPTER 9

IMPROVING KEY KNOWLEDGE WORK CAPABILITIES

"The single greatest challenge facing managers
in the developed countries of the world
is to raise the productivity of knowledge and service workers.
This challenge, which will dominate the management agenda
for the next several decades,
will ultimately determine the competitive performance of companies.
Even more important,
it will determine the very fabric of society
and the quality of life in every industrialized nation."

Peter F. Drucker
American management guru

Information technology apparently has an important role to play as an enabler of new and smarter ways of working. Given the potential that lies in improving knowledge worker productivity, it is a paradox that we often have access to better technology as consumers than we have as employees. By adopting new technology, we are changing our behaviors as consumers. But when we go to work, we stick to our old habits, whether we want it or not.

As consumers we have gotten used to being able to perform tasks and have access to information and resources on the go. Convenient capabilities have changed our behaviors as consumers, such as how we look for and use information and the way we carry out our tasks. We also bring these new behaviors to work, along with our devices and online services. We have discovered the benefits of seamless working from any device, allowing us to work from anywhere at any time.

For example, a project manager might begin writing a status report using an app on her tablet at home, then leave for work and continue working on the status report while on the subway, using an app on her smartphone that is connected to the same service as her tablet. When she arrives at the office she finalizes the status report, using a desktop app or web application, on her laptop.

In many ways we are more powerful today as consumers than we are as employees. As a result, we are often willing to pay from our own pockets for tools we need at work. Commercial software and devices play a 'survival of the fittest' game where the most usable and attractive win. At work, software and devices 'win' for other reasons, but instead of reducing complexity and simplifying our digital work environment, they often do the opposite.

People have to spend a lot of time and energy on useless things at work, and they know it. They even know what could be done about it. This isn't just frustrating and demoralizing for employees, but it hurts overall efficiency, productivity, and innovation. To improve the productivity of a growing workforce of knowledge worker requires a different approach to the traditional technology-centric and rationalization-focused approach. If organizations continue in the same tracks as they have so far, for every IT investment that is made the situation for knowledge workers and their productivity will get worse. This is the exact opposite to what most decision-makers believe will happen when they decide about new investments in enterprise software.

THE KNOWLEDGE WORKER'S DAILY CHALLENGES

During a knowledge worker's day, a lot of time is spent on activities such as searching for information, trying to figure out what colleagues are doing and when to contribute, re-creating information that already exists somewhere else, and so on. One might say we are spending a lot of our time at work just getting ready to work. There is plenty of waste hidden in our daily work, much of which we accept as 'normal' ways of working. Some common types of waste in knowledge work are illustrated in figure 38.

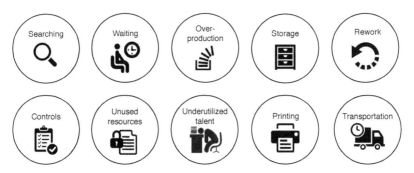

Figure 38: Common types of waste ain knowledge work

Let's see what kinds of waste that might exist in our daily work by taking a meeting as an example.

1. SEARCHING

To prepare for the upcoming meeting, you want to look at a report. You have read the report before, but you don't remember where it is. So you try to search for it on the intranet, but the report is nowhere to be found. After a while you give up and try searching for it in your email inbox instead. After some searching, you are lucky to find it. The report had been attached to a mail you received some time back. The time you spent searching is waste unless you discovered or learned something valuable in the process.

2. REWORK

You are preparing a presentation for the meeting. You were planning to reuse slides and graphics from a presentation you created for a similar meeting some time back, but after searching for it for a while you give up. You reach the painful conclusion you will need to create the presentation from scratch. The time you spend on re-creating the parts of the presentation that could have been reused from the old presentation is waste unless you came up with something much better when you re-create it.

3. WAITING

While you are working on the presentation, you discover that you lack an important piece of information to proceed with the presentation. You know that a colleague has the information, so you send her an email asking for it. Your colleague seems to work on other things and you do not know when to expect an answer. While you're waiting, you cannot proceed with the presentation. So you try to find another task to work on. Later, you receive a reply with the information you asked for. So you cease the task you just started and go back to complete the presentation. The time you spend waiting that you cannot use for other productive tasks is waste, and so is the 'downtime' that occurs when you are interrupted or switch between tasks.

4. TRANSPORTATION

The meeting you are supposed to attend will be held at another office. So you have to travel and block time in your calendar for travel time. The meeting could just have been carried out online. You already know the people you will meet, and it is a meeting where you will present and the participants will get the chance to ask you some questions. The time spent traveling, and any associated costs are waste.

5. OVERPRODUCTION

During the meeting, one participant is assigned to take notes. The person records almost every word that you said during your presentation as well as the discussion that followed. All that needed to be in the meeting notes were the important things that weren't already covered in your presentation. All the time spent on documenting more than that is waste. So is the time others need to spend on reading irrelevant information or trying to find the important information in the meeting notes.

6. STORAGE

The meeting organizer sends the meeting notes and the presentation from the meeting to all participants as attachments via email. This means that a copy of each file is created for each recipient. All the disk space that these copies occupy is waste.

7. PRINTING

Some of the participants are not comfortable reading the meeting notes and presentation on their screens, so they print these on paper. All the costs associated with printing, such as the cost for the paper and environmental costs for producing the paper, is waste.

8. UNUSED RESOURCES

The information in the presentation could be useful to many other colleagues. Since there is no easy way to share it and it is locked in the participants' email inboxes, no one else gets the chance to access. The potential uses of the presentation that never will happen can be considered as waste.

How come organizations don't do more to reduce this kind of waste? One explanation might be that it is hard to observe the waste in knowledge work. For example, it is hard to see how much time people spend on searching for information, reading and organizing incoming emails, or when a certain expertise or opportunity hasn't been fully used. Therefore, a key challenge is to make knowledge work more visible. We also have to learn how to recognize what activities are waste and what activities might create value.

OLD IMPROVEMENT STRATEGIES NO LONGER APPLY

Most business and organizational development focuses on creating structures for organizing activities and resources and then optimizing these structures for efficiency and economies of scale. This top-down approach to designing organizations, processes, and systems has worked well for industrial processes, such as supply, manufacturing, and distribution processes, as well as for more transaction-oriented processes, such as procurement and billing.

But cognitive and non-routine work is something different. Not the least because the structure of the work emerges as the work proceeds. The structure of the work cannot be defined in advance, nor can the coordination that the work will require. The people best suited to define and create this emerging structure are the people involved in the actual work, not management. This is only one aspect why traditional approaches fail when applying them to knowledge work, and why there is a strong need for new approaches and methods for business and organizational development for knowledge-intensive organizations.

Although the tasks knowledge workers need to perform come in all shapes and sizes, many of them rely on several basic capabilities, such as finding information or locating expertise. There are numerous examples of how important these capabilities are, and how much waste is generated when they are weak. For example, as a motivation for their investment in social technologies, Intel estimated that their employees spent one day per week on trying to find information and locating the expertise they needed to do their job (Buczek, 2009). McKinsey (2012) estimated that employees, on average, spend over 9 hours per week searching and gathering information.

Some types of waste are easy to measure and estimate. But for the costs of not finding information, or the costs associated with finding and acting on the wrong information, these are much harder to make visible and estimate. Although time wasted is a powerful measure since it can be easily understood, one can assume that weak capabilities lead to even more serious consequences, such as lost innovations, sub-optimization, lack of reuse, and quality problems.

HOW TO IMPROVE KNOWLEDGE WORK CAPABILITIES

Improving basic knowledge work capabilities can reduce a lot of the waste in knowledge work. This requires both developing new ways of working and introducing new or improved digital technology as is illustrated in figure 39. An organization that doesn't introduce new digital technology nor develops new ways of working will only preserve the status quo and see no improvements. Throwing new tools at employees, as technology-centric organizations often do, without actively developing new ways of working, will only pave cow paths. In the digital world, 'paving cow paths' means that you digitalize paths shaped by existing behaviors instead of thinking how digital technology can enable smarter paths.

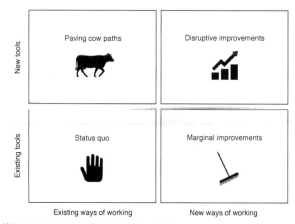

Figure 39: Ways to develop better ways of working

A better strategy is to continuously improve ways of working. Improving ways of working while keeping existing tools can also lead to improvements. For example, by using a document template with instructions on how to write meeting notes, writing overly long meeting notes can be avoided. People can also be taught how to organize their email inboxes so that it will be easier to find the information they receive or send to others. The people who print information out of habit can be asked not to print unless it is necessary and instead read it on their screens. If all of these small improvements were aggregated, the improvement in terms of time and money saved would likely be substantial.

Yet, it is by developing new ways of working and introducing new tools that an organization can see huge or even disruptive improvements to knowledge worker productivity. If the meeting notes were written on a wiki page (or intranet page) instead of in a Word document, and the presentation would be attached to the meeting notes, then no storage would be wasted. If people could access the wiki page and the presentation from their mobile devices or private computer at home, it wouldn't be necessary to print it to read it while commuting or when at home. And since both the meeting notes and the presentation are stored within a platform that is accessible and searchable, the meeting participants would know where to search for it, and other colleagues who might have use for the presentation can access it, which is not the case if it is locked in people's email inboxes.

NINE BASIC KNOWLEDGE WORK CAPABILITIES

The simplest way to define a capability is to say that it is the ability to do something. It is a combination of processes, information, people, and tools that enables you to perform a certain task. For example, the capability you have to write a report will be very different if you write it on a typewriter or using a computer with word processing software (see figure 40).

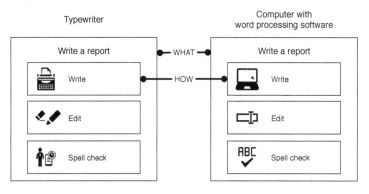

Figure 40: The capability to write a report

To write the report you will need to compose, edit, format, and correct the spelling and grammar of the report. A primitive way to provide this capability would be offer you a typewriter, a pack of 100 sheets of paper, Tipp-Ex for correcting mistakes, and someone to review the spelling and grammar.

If offered a computer with word processing software that includes features such as automatic formatting and automatic spelling and grammar-checking, chances are you will be much more capable of creating high-quality information. Or to put it another way, if you need a hole in the wall, wouldn't you rather use an electric drill than a hand drill? The outcome is the same, but the capability is much stronger due to new technology.

If you improve a capability, it means people will be empowered to perform their tasks more efficiently and effectively. Since a capability is typically used for executing tasks in many contexts, a small improvement of a capability can create substantial improvement when aggregated on process, department, and enterprise levels.

Regardless of what industry an organization is operating in, a set of nine capabilities can be considered as a foundation for performing collaborative knowledge work (see figure 41).

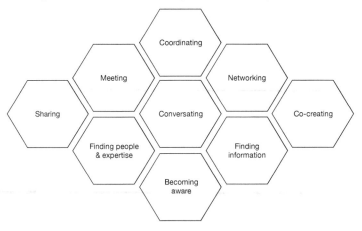

Figure 41: The Knowledge Work Capabilities Framework

BECOMING AWARE

Becoming aware is about creating workspace awareness. It is about your ability to monitor and keep track of what's happening at your workspace; who is doing what, who is interacting with whom, whose turn it is to contribute, and so on. It is essential to have workspace awareness to collaborate with other people.

Many people work in large or dispersed organizations. They need to spend a lot of time and energy to become aware of what is happening elsewhere. They might know a bit about what is happening in their close proximity, but they increasingly work and interact with more people than ever before, many of whom are separated from them by time or space.

The distribution of teams and the isolation of teams from the rest of the workforce lead to a decreased workspace awareness. This not only makes it hard to collaborate in teams, but also to coordinate the efforts and decisions of different teams. Team opacity limits both the implicit communication between members and the communication between the team and the rest of the workforce. It also impedes the development of trust, cohesion, and engagement, all of which are fundamental to efficient and effective collaboration within teams and between individual workers or teams within an enterprise.

If we compare this to when people work together face-to-face at the same physical location and can see what colleagues are doing and overhear conversations, it's not hard to see that there is room for improvement.

FINDING PEOPLE AND EXPERTISE

As work becomes increasingly interdependent, complex, and unpredictable, we rely more and more on external information and other people's expertise. Finding an expert is a critical task in modern enterprises. We need it for handling exceptions, solving problems, making the right decisions and so forth. It is hard and requires a lot of effort to find the right expertise. The cost of not finding an expert can be significant – lost opportunities, unhappy customers, duplicate work, and sub-optimization.

Research shows that knowledge workers often use as much as 40 percent of their time to find answers, something which also has been confirmed by in-house research at companies such as Pfizer (Cohen, 2010) and Intel (Buczek and Harkins, 2009). More than half of this time is trying to find answers that others in the company already have. This implies that effective 'people findability' can be more important than document search, especially in large organizations where you don't know what person has the skills or knowledge you need.

In most large organizations it is hard to find out who knows what or who has a certain expertise. Sometimes, the only way to find out is to get to know people and ask them who they know that might have a certain expertise. Since we usually get to know the people we work with or are in our close proximity, we ask those persons for answers instead of asking someone we don't know that has a potentially better answer. The tools we have at hand to do this are often inefficient, making it a cumbersome and time-consuming task to locate the expertise we need. Often, the expertise we really need is hidden or out of reach of our social networks and tools.

FINDING INFORMATION

Information is the raw material of knowledge work. Since we need new information to create value, it is natural that we spend a lot of our time looking for potentially useful information. When we do, there are often so many places to look, many of which we don't even have access to. And if we aren't aware that a specific piece of information exists in the first place, how can we possibly discover it and ask for permission to use it? How can we find out what information exists to begin with unless someone tells us about it? We can't. Paradoxically, we live in an age of information abundance and constantly battle with the feeling of information overload, at the same time as we suffer from a lack of information.

SHARING

Knowledge not shared is knowledge lost. When employees don't share what they know with each other, the knowledge stays with them and leaves the company when they leave.

"Sharing" is an asynchronous type of communication where you create content such as text, graphics or video to transmit information to those who might have a need for it or could find it usable. You rarely know if or when it will be used and often not by whom it will be used. Ideas, knowledge and experiences are typical things you share in this way.

When we openly share what we know, others can take part and help to develop and maintain a much richer body of knowledge than we possess ourselves. When we share and use our knowledge we create something together; the results will in most cases be much better than we could have accomplished on our own.

When the only ways that we can rapidly share ideas and information with coworkers is to pick up the phone or email, how do we share something when we don't have any names to put on the list of recipients? To publish it on a traditional intranet is out of the question if the information isn't of general value. If we put it in a document on a file server, it most likely won't be discovered, found, or used by people who need it.

So how do we help other people access the information we possess? How can we access information they might possess and that might be invaluable to us even though we don't know it yet?

Efficient and effective communication and conversations between people are the lifeblood of modern organizations. Plenty of research has shown that the more people communicate, the better. An MIT study by Pentland showed that 40 percent of the productivity of creative teams is directly related to the amount of communication they have with others to discover, gather, and internalize information.

CONVERSATING

Conversating is when two or more or more people have a conversation. If information is the lifeblood of an organization, then conversations make the information flow. Conversations help people quickly reach a mutual understanding, build workplace awareness, exchange tacit knowledge, and build relationships. What starts as an informal conversation might end up in collaboration.

CO-CREATING

Creating an information record is something we need to do whenever we cannot communicate directly with someone face-to-face, or when the information we exchange needs to be captured explicitly. Creating information is rarely a solitary task today. In a knowledge-intensive organization, employees need to co-create new information instead of solely contributing input and/or advice in the creation process. Co-creation also plays an important role for building culture and community, and so is an important capability for organizations to develop.

MEETING

A meeting is a situation where two or more people meet at a certain place. It can be planned or spontaneous, taking place in real life or via communication technology. The more distributed and specialized the workforce becomes, the harder it becomes for individuals to meet in person. The greater our workloads, the less space we have in our calendars to meet.

Paradoxically, as work is becoming increasingly interdependent, we need to have more meetings with more people. We all know that many of the meetings that we attend are not efficient. Sometimes no agenda is distributed in advance. Sometimes people who were not invited show up. Other times the discussions get off the track. More often than not, the meeting time is exceeded. All too often, actions are not identified and action plans not created or communicated. Afterwards, actions are forgotten and never carried out.

To make meetings efficient, you can come a long way just by following basic ground rules on how to facilitate efficient meetings. But there is also a lot that can be improved when it comes to how you communicate with the meeting participants and stakeholders, how you perform online meetings, and how you create, manage, and distribute any information related to the meeting.

NETWORKING

Networking is about being able to connect and interact with others to exchange information and develop professional or social relationships. Networking significantly impacts our individual performance and our collective performance as an organization. Our social networks are also very important to the information system in an organization as these networks "strongly influence information diffusion … and access to novel information" (Aral, Brynjolfsson & Van Alstyne, 2007).

Since information diffusion in organizations follows the structure of our relationships, having access to the right tools for building and maintaining relationships and for disseminating information through our social networks can have significant impact on the effectiveness of an organization.

Coordination is about organizing and managing the interaction and dependencies between people and other resources to fulfill a specific goal. It is a key capability in all situations where the work of two or more people is interdependent, whether it concerns an activity, project, or process. In *ad hoc* knowledge work, coordination is something every participant does, continuously. It happens implicitly as each individual tries to anticipate what their team members are doing and what they need and when. Thus, coordination depends strongly on workplace awareness.

CHAPTER 10

CLIMBING
THE COLLABORATION
PYRAMID

"Communication leads to community,
that is, to understanding,
intimacy and mutual valuing."

Rollo May
American existential psychologist

In a small company comprising a couple of dozen people working at the same location, everybody knows everybody. For people located within sight and hearing distance of each other, it is fairly easy for them to become aware of what their colleagues are doing. Even if people spend most of their time at their computers doing 'invisible' stuff such as word processing or programming, the barrier to interact and start an informal conversation is low due to the short physical distance between them.

A quick chat when you fetch a coffee, or a discussion during lunch, is likely to happen frequently. Even those who don't actively take part in a conversation are likely to overhear what it is about and join in if they find it relevant. The cocktail party effect allows people to tune in and tune out from conversations in a room, focusing their attention on those that interest them, while filtering out most of the rest.

What starts as an informal conversation about a problem during lunch might evolve into a collaborative effort to solve it after lunch. Anyone that has the required time, expertise, and motivation to work on the problem can do so. As soon as they have developed a good enough understanding of the problem, created a hypothesis for the solution, and figured out what it takes to start working on the solution, they can delegate tasks and responsibilities within the team. A team has formed, and now it is all about execution and coordinating activities. A team that didn't exist before lunch is now fully operational, and the problem might just get solved in the same afternoon. In a small company, teams often self-mobilize this way.

MOBILIZING THE POWER OF THE MANY

Over the years, a great studies have looked at how groups can improve their performance. More recently the focus has shifted to team performance.

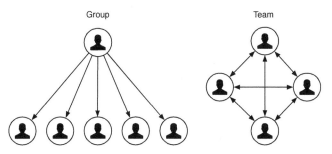

Figure 42: The main difference between a group and a team is in the coordination

A group can be defined as a number of people who work with quite independent tasks (figure 42). The individuals handle their own tasks and performance. In case their work needs to be coordinated, a manager or supervisor usually does it. When the members interact it is typically for exchanging information, helping each other out, or socializing.

A team comprises several people whose work is highly interdependent and where they work closely together to achieve a goal. They often share responsibility and accountability for the work they do as a team, which includes making decisions, solving problems, and coordinating their work. Therefore, they meet and interact frequently to coordinate their efforts.

As work is becoming more and more complex and interdependent, the focus of performance improvement efforts is shifting from organizational groups to cross-functional teams. Groups cannot address many of the problems, threats, ideas, and opportunities that require collaborative action. These might require capabilities that can only be mobilized by cross-organizational collaboration efforts, involving anything from a few people to hundreds or even thousands of people. An organization must be able to quickly mobilize and organize people from any part of the organization into teams, and the teams need to be scalable to match the problem or opportunity at hand.

Teams can self-mobilize also in large and dispersed organizations, but it is more likely to happen within organizational groups than across groups and locations. As soon as an idea or problem requires the collaboration of people with different expertise and skill sets, or requires more people than is available in the organizational group, people from multiple organizational groups usually need to get involved. In such a situation it is not likely that the team will emerge by itself.

EXISTING SOLUTIONS TO MOBILIZE TEAMS FAIL

Most companies have invested much more into making teams perform well once they have formed than in how to quickly mobilize and organize teams of any composition and size. Everyone who has ever worked in a group of some sort has most likely been subject to team building activities, but how many have been given the opportunity to practice how to quickly mobilize and organize a team of people coming from anywhere? Not many at all.

This reflects the emphasis put on performance and optimization at the expense of responsiveness, agility, and innovation. Mobilizing and organizing groups and teams has been the responsibility of management, carried out by doing anything from changing roles or positions to making large reorganizations. But the high transaction costs of the traditional bureaucratic organization make such solutions inefficient. Instead, organizations need to look into other solutions, especially solutions that allow them to use the *power of the many*.

There are likely formal processes and systems in place that have helped pick the right people for a team. Or the organization relies on people, such as managers, who have connections in other teams who they can ask to recommend candidates. The process of forming the team will take time, and it will rely on specific individuals acting as brokers, or on systems that aim to streamline the matching process and can only provide results as good as the data that have been entered into them.

These solutions are often blunt and ineffective for finding and mobilizing the best people for a specific task or goal. It is unlikely that the people involved in the matching process will have enough understanding of the problem, or which people have the right skills, knowledge, motivations, social skills, and so forth to be best suited to work on the task or goal. Under such conditions teams don't get formed over lunch, and problems don't get solved in the same afternoon. That is why organizations need to enable teams to self-mobilize.

WHERE SELF-MOBILIZED TEAMS COME FROM

Self-organized teams don't come from nowhere. They emerge from conversations between people, such as the spontaneous conversation between colleagues during lunch when someone brings up a problem he or she has just discovered. And for such conversations to take place, people need places to meet or bump into each other.

Again we have the curse of physical proximity. When we are close, we are more likely to have those open, frequent, spontaneous, and informal conversations that keep us well informed and make collaboration happen naturally. When we aren't close, the likelihood that such conversations will take place decreases dramatically.

In a large organization everybody cannot know everybody. To start with, there is a cognitive limit to how many people someone can maintain relationships with. Robert Dunbar, a British anthropologist, estimated that humans could maintain around 150 stable relationships ("Dunbar's number", 2015).

> "As group size grows, a dizzying amount of data must be processed. A group of five has a total of 10 bilateral relationships between its members; a group of 20 has 190;

a group of 50 has 1,225. Such a social life requires a big neocortex, the layers of neurons on the surface of the brain, where conscious thought takes place. In his 1992 paper, Dunbar plotted the size of the neocortex of each type of primate against the size of the group it lived in: The bigger the neocortex, the larger the group a primate could handle. At the same time, even the smartest primate—us—doesn't have the processing power to live in an infinitely large group. To come up with a predicted human group size, Dunbar plugged our neocortex ratio into his graph and got 147.8."

Bennett (2013)

Furthermore, most people don't get the chance to meet, connect, and get to know many people in other organizational groups or at other locations. Unless they have been picked to be on the same team, or know each other from before, it is unlikely they will be able to spend the time with each other it takes to get to know one another.

THE COLLABORATION PYRAMID

The collaboration pyramid model is intended as a tool that will help organizations understand what they need to do to make collaboration happen naturally across groups and locations, and to increase the effectiveness of collaboration efforts. The model, illustrated in figure 43, comprises eight layers, building on each other from the bottom upwards. The most fundamental activities for collaboration are at the bottom of the pyramid. This makes it easy to draw a parallel to Maslow's hierarchy of needs, which is often represented as a pyramid.

Figure 43: The collaboration pyramid model

The top three layers represent activities we typically think of as parts of structured team-based collaboration, such as forming the team, coordinating activities, and carrying out the actual activities. These are often formalized, visible, measured, and evaluated, just as the result that the team produces.

The activities in the five lower layers are activities of a more social nature, not bound to a particular collaboration effort, such as people introducing themselves to each other, having informal conversations, connecting, creating and sharing information with each other, and so forth. Things that happen on a daily basis, naturally embedded in daily work.

The model doesn't say that the activities in the lower layers are simpler or less complex that the activities in the upper layers. Rather, it is the other way around. Complex social interaction and relationship building activities are needed for people to form teams and collaborate. The activities in these layers happen naturally when people are in close proximity and interact face-to-face.

When people are close, it is easy to be introduced to each other and to spontaneously meet or go and talk to each other. What begins as an informal and spontaneous conversation might then evolve into a collaboration effort. But as soon as people are located more than 50 feet away from each other, the likelihood they will meet and have an informal and spontaneous conversation drops dramatically. And so does the likelihood that collaboration will happen naturally. To enable collaboration to happen naturally across groups and locations, an organization must help its employees perform the activities in the five lower layers across teams and locations.

The collaboration pyramid illustrates a problem common within large and distributed organizations – the activities in the five lower layers are hard to scale beyond organizational groups and geographic locations. If people have ties to people in other groups, then some communication and collaboration might happen spontaneously across groups even though it is less common than among people within the same group at the same location. The problem is that, in a large and dispersed organization, most people don't get the chance to develop relationships with people outside their own groups. Hence their social networks are often limited to people that belong to the same organizational group and to people in their close proximity.

People who perform well in the lower levels often have high visibility in the organizational chart, either as managers or formally appointed experts. They often have the required resources and mandate to invest in social activities. The problem is that these people are usually not the only ones who need strong social networks to solve complex problems. They are not the only ones who might have ideas that could lead to new innovations.

Anyone who is confronted with a problem benefits from having a strong social network when trying to solve it. Ideas can come from anywhere and if the person with the idea has a strong social network, it is more likely that it will be discovered and taken up.

STANDING ON THE SHOULDERS OF GIANTS

A modern interpretation of the Western metaphor about the dwarfs standing on the shoulders of giants is that each new discovery that is made builds on previous discoveries. In the context of enterprises and collaboration, one can say that each person who creates value builds on the value created by other people. Each individual, team, or group is a dwarf, and the giants whose shoulders they stand upon is the workforce as a collective, past and present. The better the workforce operates as a collective and the better it can keep any past contributions alive, the taller and stronger are the giants, and the more value an individual, team or group that stands on their shoulders can create. This holds true not only for the performance of individuals, but also for the performance of teams and collaboration efforts.

What we see when we think of collaboration in the traditional sense (structured team-based collaboration), is the tip of the iceberg of all the cooperative and collaborative efforts that take place within in an organization or enterprise. Besides the collaboration that takes part through highly repeatable processes, there is a lot of more *ad hoc* activities and collaborative efforts that bring value in organizations. Most of these are invisible to most people, including management. Just as a lot of the waste in knowledge-intensive organizations is hidden, so is much of the value-creation.

For example, we rarely see many of the activities that precede a collaborative effort, or the activities that external people perform to help a team. We also rarely see the other things that have been critical for the team's success, such as how individual members have used their personal networks to access knowledge, information, and skills they needed, some of which are likely to have been instrumental to the team's success.

If we take a look at the collaboration pyramid model in figure 44 , there is a 'water line' separating activities that typically have a high visibility in organizations from those that are less visible.

Figure 44: A lot of activities happen 'below the surface'

Most of the activities in the lower 5 layers happen 'below the surface'. Management seldom give any attention to these activities, at least not beyond their own teams, and some even regard them as waste, not work. These activities are usually not visible, recognized, or valued by organizations. Yet, these activities are fundamental both for collaboration to happen, and for a lot of other value-creation to take place. Below the surface you will find:

- activities that allow people to get to know each other, build relationships, and understand what others can contribute.
- direct and indirect contributions from people outside the team – by the extended team, stakeholders, and external contributors.
- ongoing community building that makes people build trust in each other and commit themselves to a shared purpose.
- efforts of gaining the workspace awareness necessary for making the right decisions in any collaborative effort.

It is reasonable to assume that a substantial part of value-creation activities is hidden because many of these activities are too small to be observed and measured. For example, someone might help a colleague in another team to find a piece of information, maybe just by sharing a link or pointing to a source of information. In most cases, such an activity won't leave any trace or pop up on anyone else's radar screen. The same thing goes for answering a question, adding metadata to content so it is easier to find, or updating a piece of incorrect data.

These small tasks, what I sometimes call 'tiny work', do not pop up on management's radar. What they see is just the time and resources people spent on something that appears to be nothing, making it look like waste, as an invisible productivity drain around which routine activities orbit like stars around a black hole. As the amount of cognitive non-routine work increases, the drain will appear to grow bigger and bigger. A lot of value-creating activities will wrongly be mistaken for waste.

SURFACING TINY WORK

A great challenge for organizations is to make these activities visible. The concept of 'Working Out Loud', originally mentioned by Bryce Williams in 2010, is about this. By enabling and encouraging people to continuously and openly narrate their work, using social media platforms, it can be made observable to others ("Working Out Loud", 2015). When it is becomes visible, it can also be used by more people and thus create more value. John Stepper defines the concept:

> *"Working Out Loud starts with making your work visible in such a way that it might help others. When you do that – when you work in a more open, connected way – you can build a purposeful network that makes you more effective and provides access to more opportunities."*

> *John Stepper. Author of "Working Out Loud"*

Due to the low visibility of knowledge work, a lot of information, knowledge, and talent are put to waste. For example, when people exchange information about what they are working on via email, there is virtually zero visibility to anyone who doesn't receive that email. Some people try to inform potential stakeholders by putting them on the CC list, but doing so they generate occupational spam and information glut. If the communication and information that is exchanged, such as the status of tasks or digital content that people have produced, would instead be shared on an open platform, then work would become much more visible. You can find out what people are working on, what they have produced, or what problems they might be occupied with instead of having to ask them directly (if you have such a relationship).

To avoid having value-creating activities mistaken for waste, we need to develop a better understanding of what activities create value and why. We need to dig deep enough to see that many activities from a distance appear to be trivial or distractions are sometimes prerequisites for value-creation. In many organizations, social activities among employees are still treated as unwanted distractions and productivity drains, even though they are essential for collaboration and employee engagement.

NETWORKS AND COMMUNITIES COME BEFORE TEAMS

We can see that the bottom five layers of the collaboration pyramid model are very much about social networking and community building.

Communities connect the talent of experts and professionals and drive engagement around topics, ideas, problems, products, and initiatives. Collaboration happens more naturally within groups than between groups because people that belong to the same group are usually part of the same community. They share the same interests or characteristics. They share the same leader or manager. If people in a community will benefit from cooperating, they most likely will, and they will be more open to collaborate.

When people who don't belong to the same community are to cooperate or collaborate, things become much harder. It doesn't mean it cannot happen, or that people won't contribute or collaborate with people from other communities. It's just that people have much stronger intrinsic motivation, such as belonging, recognition, and identity, to contribute and collaborate with members of their own community than they have with external people. To collaborate with external people, they need to have more incentives.

It cannot be overstated how important communities are for communication and collaboration in organizations. If you have a strong and vibrant community of autonomous people, teams can build themselves. So first you build the community, then you build the teams you need.

WORKING YOUR WAY UP TO THE SURFACE

The collaboration pyramid can also be used to understand what an individual needs to do to become part of a community, to contribute, and to get involved in collaborative efforts. Let's see how you would work your way up the pyramid if you were to join a new organization and want to put yourself to good use as soon as possible, intending to become engaged in collaborative efforts. We will just assume that you are committed to the purpose of the organization and that you share the values that underpin the organization's culture. Besides your skills and knowledge, you also bring with you an amount of self-awareness, autonomy, and motivation.

MAKING YOURSELF VISIBLE

The first thing you have to do is to make yourself visible to others. If you never introduce yourself to people, if you avoid people and hide in a corner at the office, no one will notice you are there, much less ask for your help or involve you in any collaborative work.

To make yourself visible, you have to introduce yourself and take part in different contexts where you are given the opportunity to communicate and interact with other people. People have to know that you are there, and where they can find you.

In a small organization this is usually not a problem, but if the organization is larger than a few dozen people and is distributed in two or more locations, it will be a challenge. The larger and more distributed the organization, the greater this challenge will be. This applies to the activities in all layers of the collaboration pyramid. When you make yourself visible, it puts you in motion towards potential collaborators.

SHARE WHAT YOU KNOW, HAVE, THINK AND DO

Once people know your name and can put a face to your name, you need to make them aware of what you know and what you are capable of, your expertise and skills. This is what you do in the second layer of the collaboration pyramid. It is all about making people understand how and where you can create value and contribute to the shared purpose. If you also share your beliefs and ideas, people will get the chance to know you as a person, and perhaps see that you can bring something new to their work. You should be open with what information you bring with you, and inform them about your current activities. It might apply to the work your colleagues are doing.

When you share and engage in conversations, you learn important things about your colleagues and the organization. You will attract others who share your interests, or are interested in seeing how the things you bring can benefit their work.

FIND AND DISCOVER PEOPLE

The third layer of the collaboration pyramid is where you actively try to find and discover interesting people to interact with, which can mean anything from sharing information to collaborating.

This requires that your colleagues have done the same thing you have: if they haven't made themselves visible, exposing as much relevant information as they can about themselves, you won't be able to find or discover people to interact with. If they do, chances are you will figure out who a person is, evaluate if it would be beneficial to get to know them, and get enough information to feel confident in contacting and interacting with him.

COMMUNICATE AND CONNECT

When you have contacted and started interacting with a person, you begin to get to know each other and build trust in each other. You develop a relationship. This is what you do on the fourth level of the collaboration pyramid. If the person is in close proximity or on your team, chances are you will develop a strong and ongoing relationship. You won't get to know most people you meet well, resulting in weaker and non-persistent relationships; but being able to reconnect in the future might be useful to you or those people.

CONTRIBUTE

When you have started building a personal network, you can start contributing for real. If you share information with colleagues in your network, chances are pretty good they will trust and make use of the information because they trust you.

As you might have figured, this is not a linear and sequential process but an iterative and parallel process. We do things on all layers of the collaboration pyramid at the same time, but the hierarchy is still important. One thing leads to the other, as it all starts at the bottom even though things you do further up can strengthen the underpinning layers.

For example, if you or your team makes a valuable contribution and get recognized for it, your visibility will likely increase, exposing you to more collaboration opportunities.

The more we support people to travel up in the collaboration pyramid, the more collaboration opportunities they will be exposed to and might contribute to. The problem is that activities in the lower five layers are usually not well supported, and people working in a large and distributed organization will be defeated by the challenges and blocks, and stay in their organizational silos. The first step towards improving real enterprise-wide collaboration is to recognize the existence and value of these five layers and give them the proper support.

REMOVING BARRIERS TO ENTERPRISE COLLABORATION

The performance of an individual or team depends a lot on the cooperation by individuals and teams within the community when it takes place in a dynamic, unpredictable, and complex environment. There isn't necessarily a much weaker dependency in a more static, predictable, and simple environment. But under these circumstances many of the dependencies can be anticipated and managed. This is often done by creating and maintaining structures such as a hierarchical organization, processes and systems. Even if something out of the ordinary happens, there is likely a procedure to follow and structures in place to ensure that the procedure is followed in the right way. When the operational environment is more dynamic, unpredictable and complex, then more and more of the work that needs to be carried out cannot be anticipated. The appropriate structures cannot be defined and set up in advance. The structures will have to quickly emerge as needed and then dissolve just as fast.

For enterprise-wide collaboration to happen, the community building and cooperation must stretch beyond any barriers such as organizations, time, and place. Groupthink and organizational silos cannot be allowed to limit the ability for one or several organizations to collaborate as an enterprise. If the enterprise as a whole is not one single community, and if people don't cooperate freely within and across organizations involved in the enterprise, enterprise collaboration cannot happen efficiently and effectively.

CHAPTER 11

SHAPING A NEW COMMUNICATION CULTURE

"Trust is the bandwidth of communication."

Karl-Erik Sveiby
Professor in Knowledge Management

Our ability to collaborate depends heavily on how we communicate. Consequently, we can create better conditions for collaboration efforts to be successful by improving the way we communicate with each other. There are five principles that help to bring about more effective communication in an organization: openness, transparency, participation, conversation, and recognition (figure 45).

Figure 45: Five principles for achieving effective communication

These five principles should be applied when designing digital tools and the entire digital work environment. The principles should also be considered when designing performance metrics, management practices, processes, and ways of working. This is because aspects of the organization must encourage and enable collaborative attitudes and behaviors. Communication cultures that build on these five principles provide the foundation for creating a more collaborative culture and reaping the benefits of collaboration.

OPENNESS

Information has no value if it cannot be used. Openness, which is about not concealing information, is thus a prerequisite for getting the maximum value from a piece of information.

Many organizations are characterized by a 'need to know' culture where people won't get access to information unless they explicitly ask for it. People might not think of it as concealing information, but if the information is not there to be discovered and they don't actively share it, they are in fact concealing it. Because, how do you get to know that the information exists, or where it is located in the first place, if it isn't possible to discover?

Humans have a bias against openness and open systems. Unless an organization explicitly encourages openness and sharing, a 'need to know' culture is likely to emerge. The CIA and the US State Department are two examples of organizations that have publicly announced that they are trying to transform their cultures towards increased openness, or a 'need to share' culture. In such a culture, people proactively share information they get access to and that might be valuable to others, even though they don't know for sure who will have use for it.

Openness encourages respect and participation, even across geographic and cultural boundaries. Access to knowledge empowers and motivates people to strive towards common goals together.

Let's say you would create a document with your lessons learned after having closed a project. When done, you save the document on your computer. Only you will be able to use it. No one else will know it exists unless you tell them so. Therefore it is more likely that you will make the document accessible to the other members of the project. That way, they can learn from it as well, and perhaps they will share their own lessons learned with you.

You could also go one step further. You could make the document accessible to all your colleagues, even those who you don't work with. Assuming that you work in a fairly large organization, you have colleagues who you have never even met. If you make the document accessible to all your colleagues, you will give them the chance to repeat your successes and avoid making the same mistakes as you did. Your lessons learned now have the potential to benefit anyone within your organization, far beyond your team. This is the value of openness.

Here are some ways to encourage openness:

- Make it easy for people to create information.
- Make sharing as easy as possible
- Make openness the default option. Protecting something should require an extra effort (and thought)

TRANSPARENCY

Transparency is about making sure information can be discovered and trusted. Openness and transparency are two sides of the same coin. If openness is about not concealing information from others, transparency is about making it visible. Even if a piece of information is made accessible and actively shared by someone, barriers such as geographical distance, organization hierarchies and IT systems can limit the visibility of the information. Transparency is about making these barriers see-through.

Transparency is also about traceability. Our confidence in information depends highly on the ability to trace it back to its origin. Where does it come from, and from whom? If we don't know that, chances are we won't trust it, and consequently not use it even if it is relevant and valuable. Traceability helps us build trust in both information and people. The former is essential for turning information into action, and the latter for sharing information and collaborating with each other.

Transparency also strengthens accountability. If a piece of information or action is traceable to a specific individual that individual must also stand accountable for the information and answer to anyone who questions it. On the other side of the coin, traceability allows the individual to get recognized for whatever value the information can help to create, or perhaps help the person build a reputation as an expert.

Above all, openness and transparency are fundamental for creating workplace awareness, and thus for people to spot relevant opportunities to participate.

Let's say you uploaded your lessons learned document to a folder on a file server that all your colleagues can access. Now assume that a colleague is looking for some lessons learned from a past project and finds your document. Will the person trust the information in the document enough to use it? If your name appears as the author of the document, there is a chance your colleague will trust the information, especially if he or she knows who you are. Your colleague could also contact you to check if the information really is accurate, up-to-date and complete. However, considering that you work for a large organization, it can be hard for someone who doesn't know who you are to find you based on only a name. There is also a risk someone else has made changes to the document after you put it in the shared folder. Often there is no way to tell what has been changed and by whom. If the information has been changed, it might not be accurate or complete anymore. Considering this risk, it is not unlikely that the colleague who found your document won't trust and use the information in it.

If it is perfectly clear who authored the document, if the author can be easily found and contacted and if there is a complete history of all changes made to the document, by whom, and when, then it will be easier to trust the information in the document. This is the value of transparency.

Here are some ways to encourage transparency:

- Create ways that allow people to find and discover other people and information across organizations, geography, and other barriers or structures.
- Don't allow people to be anonymous. Someone who is anonymous cannot stand accountable or be recognized for their contributions.
- Make it easy to trace information to the person that created, shared, or modified it.

PARTICIPATION

Participation is the process by which individuals, groups, and organizations are given the opportunity to join an activity. To participate is a basic human need, and by participating in various communities we develop a sense of identity, belonging, and purpose. Participation connects us to other people, gives meaning to our lives, and makes us want to have responsibilities, be assigned tasks, and cooperate with other people. People that don't get the opportunity to participate easily feel alienated, lonely, useless, and stop believing in themselves, resulting in a loss of interest and maybe even an identity crisis. Participation is fundamental for building employee engagement and productivity in organizations. Someone who participates in an activity can choose to be more or less involved; from passively observing to actively contributing or taking full responsibility for the activity. When people get involved in something, they commit themselves to it, becoming willing to invest their time, energy, reputation, or perhaps entire career and lives to make it happen. That is how people and organizations can move mountains and accomplish the seemingly impossible.

Let's return to your lessons learned document. Now that you have uploaded it to a shared folder on a file server that all your colleagues can access, anyone within your organization can now find and read the document. But you have only given them read-only access to the document. This means that it is only you who can make changes to the document. Not even the members of your project can participate and update the document with their own lessons learned. They will have to contact you and ask you to add or change information in the document. Every unnecessary step someone needs to take to participate and contribute will lower their willingness to do so.

So, you decide to give the members of your project permissions to update the document. But why not allow anyone to update the document? There might be colleagues who could make very valuable contributions, perhaps making you aware of mistakes you have made and helping you avoid repeating the same mistakes in your next project.

Here are some ways to encourage participation:

- Design systems and processes to lower the threshold to participation. Tools and technologies must make it extremely easy to communicate and interact.

- Make participation optional. Leave it to the individual to choose whether to participate.

- Enable multiple ways to participate so that people can participate in the way they prefer and are comfortable with. Some will want to actively contribute – others might just want to passively observe.

- Do not exclude people unless absolutely necessary and never exclude people by default.

CONVERSATION

A conversation is when two or more people exchange information. It is interactive since each new communication episode builds on the previous. A conversation can be about anything, and it is often spontaneous and unpredictable.

A conversation is two-way communication, and people prefer that to one-way communication. It enables them to communicate more effectively, to reach mutual understanding about something, and therefore arrive at the right decisions faster, identifying the right actions to take. That is why face-to-face meetings, phone calls, and emails are so popular in business. People need to have free-form, interactive and rich conversations on equal terms to communicate efficiently and effectively with each other, achieving the desired outcome. Free-form, interactive, and rich conversations also help to create virtual proximity in situations where people are physically apart, which makes them more prone to exchange information and collaborate with each other.

There was a time when employees weren't expected to talk or think. The extreme repeatability and clear division of tasks by the assembly line made talking and thinking unnecessary. Workers should just comply with orders and follow procedures.

These times are passing. Work is a conversation, and this is certainly true for non-routine and highly interdependent work. People that work together in a team need to talk to each other frequently, whether to coordinate their actions, make decisions, analyze information, or solve problems. Conversations also connect people in different teams, helping them to access new information and knowledge, as well as to find opportunities to collaborate. Returning to the example with the lessons learned document, a colleague who has found and read your document might have a few questions about the information in the document. If your colleague can contact you and have a back-and-forth conversation with you, it is likely that your colleague would get the questions answered quickly. Perhaps you would learn something from the conversation as well and update your document accordingly. Who knows, since you share some mutual interest you might connect with your colleague and start an exchange that eventually will lead you collaborate on something.

Here are some ways to encourage conversation:

- Make it possible to have informal and free-form conversations.
- Provide ways to have many-to-many conversations.
- Enable rich conversations by supporting many types of content and synchronous (real-time) as well as asynchronous communication.
- Make it possible to create or share many types of digital content to fit different communication purposes
.

RECOGNITION

Recognition refers to various types of positive feedback we might receive about our contributions and efforts as employees. Recognition meets our intrinsic psychological needs for feeling appreciated. We need recognition to know that our contributions and efforts are valued and appreciated. But it goes even deeper than that. We depend on feedback from other people to develop our identities. If we fail to be recognized, we have a harder time not only to value our contributions, but also ourselves as individuals. Getting appropriate recognition is fundamental for employee engagement and productivity, especially in a knowledge-intensive organization characterized by a lot of non-routine and collaborative work.

For example, earning the respect and recognition of our peers is an important driver for sharing knowledge. Since our knowledge is closely tied to our identities, what we share and with who shapes how our peers perceive us. It is perfectly logical that we want to share our knowledge with those who need it and recognize our contributions.

The act of sharing something tells our colleagues something about us, and that we think and care about what they might be interested in. If what we share is relevant and valuable to them, they will understand that we have really tried to understand their needs and interests. Their trust in us grows. They might trust us enough to share something back or help us out in other ways. We build relationships by helping each other. When work is interdependent, this is invaluable.

If you have a closer relationship with someone, you are more likely to share information with that person. Therefore, physical and virtual proximity and organizational belonging become factors that positively influence sharing.

The colleague who found and read your document with lessons learned found it useful and wants you to know that. If there is some way for your colleague to communicate that to you, it is likely that you will appreciate it. This kind of recognition from a colleague is usually much more powerful when it is done where more people can hear or see it. It will build your reputation, what people think of you. Let's say that your boss was to tell you that you did a great job with your lessons learned document. Wouldn't the exact same words feel more worth if he or she told you in front of all your colleagues instead of in a one-on-one meeting or email?

Here are some ways to encourage recognition

- Make it possible for anyone to recognize the contributions of any of their peers.
- Provide various ways to recognize a contribution or contributor, such as liking, commenting, or praising, so that people can choose to recognize other people in the way they prefer.
- Make sure that all recognitions are public by default.

As you can see from this example, it is when you combine the five principles that the communication gets most effective.

BALANCING VALUE AND RISK

Increasing openness, transparency, participation, conversations, and recognition within an organization will improve communication and collaboration.

There are, of course, risks associated to, for example, increased openness. But when assessing and managing these risks, we must remind ourselves that most people are risk averse. The more uncertain the returns are, the less willing we are to take a risk. The indirect and sometimes invisible correlation between communication and productivity, efficiency, and innovation doesn't help in this respect. When people don't see clear and certain returns for risk taking, they will not take any risks and they will fight those that are less risk averse. Some will wave the security flag, concerned that information will fall into the wrong hands. Some will have privacy concerns as more personal information will be exposed. Some will fear that the feeling of information overload will increase.

These might all be relevant risks, but they are manageable and often insignificant when compared to the benefits of improving the foundation for communication within an organization. All these risks can be managed; they shouldn't stop us. The potential value that might come from, for example, increased transparency is often greater than the potential costs. In contrast to what many might think, greater transparency often helps reduce risk.

For example, the bankruptcy of the financial services firm Lehman Brothers in 2008 could most likely have been avoided, or at least the effects and magnitude of the bankruptcy could have been reduced, if only their large positions and losses in subprime mortgages were not hidden.

We also tend to see risks in only one direction, which is usually the direction away from the *status quo*. We fail to see that the greatest risks most organizations face lie in preserving the status quo; bad decision-making, rework and waste, inability to innovate, low productivity, disengaged employees, failure to understand and satisfy the needs and expectations of customers. These are things that might eventually put an organisation out of business.

CHAPTER 12

SUPERPOWERING PEOPLE WITH SOCIAL TECHNOLOGY

*"When companies can't really tell the difference
between the medium and the message, they get in trouble…
the medium — a blog, Twitter, the Kindle,
even the Internet itself — isn't the important thing.
It's just a way of connecting people
with things that matter to them,
and with other people who matter to them.
That is the real power, regardless of the medium."*

*Om Malik
Indian-American web and technology writer*

Anyone who has ever worked in a small and local business knows that doing business is a social thing. In a small business, all employees get to meet and interact with the customers. They know it is essential to understand and socialize with the customer to earn their trust and loyalty.

As soon as an organization grows and becomes geographically dispersed, it becomes impossible for everybody to meet and interact with customers, or for everyone to know everyone. To ensure efficiency and economies of scale as the organization grows, much of the work as possible is automated and streamlined. That includes the interactions with customers. The organization communicates with markets of anonymous consumers instead of individual consumers.

We know now that the tide is turning. The power is shifting back to consumers from the large global corporations. Consumers want organizations to treat them as individuals, not anonymous numbers. They want to get the best customer experience there is. If they don't, they will walk away and go somewhere else. They might make their voices heard on the Internet, convincing other consumers to follow them.

A NEW WAY OF THINKING ABOUT TECHNOLOGY

Social media hasn't just shifted the power of communication from the corporations to the consumers; it has also inspired a new way of thinking about information technology. It has inspired us to design information technology to support and leverage collaborative human behaviors and make better use of our collective intellectual and social capital.

By applying the thinking and principles behind social technology when we design organizations, processes, and ways of working, we can avoid a lot of the negative things that happen when an organization grows. We can use technology to enable people to achieve great things together.

With social technology we can, for example:

- Bridge structural holes to ensure that information flows between teams.
- Level out information asymmetry so people don't misuse the power of information for personal reasons, or put what is best for the enterprise aside.
- Create virtual proximity so that frequent and spontaneous communication and collaboration can happen across time and space.
- Turn an enterprise into one community that makes cooperation and collaboration happen more naturally across teams and organizational silos.
- Make talent and expertise visible and accessible to anyone who needs it wherever it may live.
- Enable teams to emerge and self-organize to deal with problems and challenges as these arise.
- Get rid of many of the transaction costs and overheads that come with the bureaucratic organization.
- Connect a disengaged and isolated workforce so they become more engaged and productive.
- Engage all stakeholders, including customers, in the development of the enterprise and its brand, products, and services.

SOCIAL TOOLS

A number of social tools, such as blogs, wikis and micro-blogging, have emerged over the years since the mid 1990s. These social tools complement rather than replace the already well-established communication technologies that exist within most organizations today, such as telephony, email, video conferencing, and traditional intranets. These existing communication technologies have their limitations when it comes to supporting highly interactive many-to-many conversations and information exchanges, especially when lots of people from different groups are involved.

In figure 45 and 46, several traditional communication tools and social tools have been mapped to the communication matrix (from chapter seven) to illustrate which tool is most suited to the kind of communication. It is clear that the sweet spot for social tools is in many-to-many interaction.

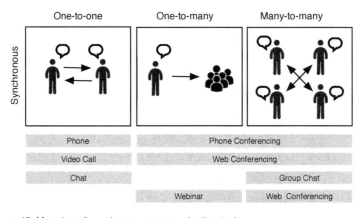

Figure 45: Mapping of synchronous communication tools

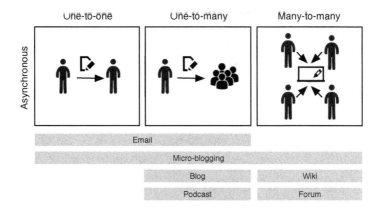

Figure 46: Mapping of asynchronous communication tools

These and other social tools help fill a gap for highly interactive many-to-many communication. Tools such as email and phone calls were designed for a linear style of communication and hence do not work well for social interaction, knowledge sharing, or collaboration.

DEFINING SOCIAL TECHNOLOGY

Social software is a category of software that supports and encourages social and collaborative behaviors. The term 'social technology; is often taken as a synonym for 'social software'. But a technology is not just about the tools. It is also the body of knowledge that is required to create the tools.

Social technology is a new way of designing software that draws knowledge from human and social sciences to leverage and extend our communication capabilities. Let's put it into perspective. Since the dawn of humanity we have invented many physical tools that extend our physical capabilities. More recently we invented computing to extend our mental capabilities. Now, with social technology, we can design tools that extend our capabilities to communicate and socialize with each other.

Social technology makes it easy for people to connect and have frequent, spontaneous, and informal communication and interaction across time and space. People can socialize with each other, chatting about what appears to be trivial stuff, even if they are not located near each other. They can get to know, and develop relationships with new people without ever meeting them face-to-face. But social technology does much more than that. It also helps us overcome some of the constraints that exist in real life when it comes to communicating, interacting, and building relationships with people.

For example, in real life it is hard to have a face-to-face conversation with more than a handful of people at the same time without risking having the conversation get out of hand. It is also hard for someone to join a conversation that has already started without interrupting the conversation and requiring a recap. With social technology, a lot more people can take part in a conversation without it becoming messy. Since the whole conversation is captured, people can jump in and out as they wish without missing out on anything.

When it comes to relationships, social technology can help us manage and maintain a much larger number of relationships than we can in real life. The Dunbar number no longer sets the limit to how many stable relationships a person can maintain.

KEY CHARACTERISTICS OF SOCIAL TECHNOLOGY

The power of social technology comes from its ability to activate and leverage our innate social needs, such as being seen and recognized for who we are, what we do, and what we know. It helps to unleash our creativity, it helps us maintain existing relationships and develop new ones, and it brings us closer to each other by allowing us to communicate on equal terms and with utmost informality and ease. All of this is essential for improving the productivity in non-routine and collaborative knowledge work. There are several characteristics of social technology that all help to make this possible.

AUTHORSHIP

Social technology is designed for freedom of expression. It enables people to create and publish their own digital content, and to do so in any context they wish to participate. If information is power, then communicating it is about using that power. Social technology gives the ability to communicate information to the people, allowing anyone to influence others.

Social technology is indifferent to formal authority, treating all people as equal in human worth and social status. Everyone has the same power to make their voices heard, and they are free to participate on equal terms in any context.

OPENNESS

Social technology enables and encourages free sharing of information and interaction across organizational, geographical, and information system silos. Social tools are designed for a greater openness than other traditional communication and collaboration tools. They are designed to be open by default. For example, when creating a space for a community, the default setting is that anyone can join the community and access whatever is shared within the community. Likewise, when people post information on a social platform, the default option is that it is accessible to all users of that platform.

TRANSPARENCY

Transparency makes the digital work environment see-through, so that one's expertise, activities, and information become visible to other people. It ensures that all contributions, conversations, and interactions can be traced to an individual. For example, being able to trace the individual who created a piece of content helps other people to trust it. It also makes it easier to recognize people for their contributions.

REACH

Something that is shared may reach all people that have access to the platform. On the Internet, it means that something can be shared with potentially everyone that has access to the Internet. Within an organization, it means that something can be shared with potentially everyone that belongs to the organization. It is up to the person who shares to limit the reach if he or she sees a reason to do so.

FREEFORM

Social technology does not predetermine the way people work together by imposing a pre-defined structure. Instead, it gives people the freedom to design and manage their work themselves, such as how they organize their work and coordinate their efforts with each other. People can communicate and interact freely with other people, they can create and use whatever types of digital content they see fit, and they can organize resources and activities as required by the work at hand. This is why social technology has such potential when it comes to supporting and improving non-routine and collaborative knowledge work.

EASE OF USE

Ease of use is an important factor in making people feel comfortable with a tool so they perceive value in using it, which leads to higher adoption. The threshold to learning and using a tool needs to be as low as possible. For example, people shouldn't need any training or have to read a manual in order use a social tool. It should be intuitive to use.

CONVERSATION

Social technology facilitates two-way communication between two or more people, i.e. conversations. Conversations help people reach mutual understanding about the things that are being communicated and are thus the lifeblood of an organization, and even more crucial in a dynamic and unpredictable business environment.

OPT IN

Although the opportunity to participate should always exist, social technology allows people to choose if they want to participate, and how. It also allows people to opt in and opt out of information flows just as they wish.

THE CONCEPT OF SOCIAL OBJECTS

The concept of social objects is central to social technology, illustrated in figure 47. A social object is a shared digital resource that can be used for sharing information or experiences about something. It can be a digital document, a video clip, a web page, a user profile, a calendar event, or any piece of digital media, which can contain various types of content such as text, images, and sound.

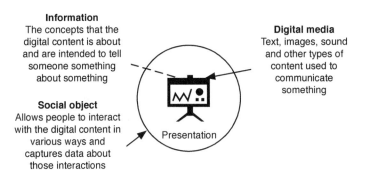

Figure 47: Defining a social object

A social object makes it possible for people to interact with digital content in the digital work environment and for the system to capture data about those interactions. Common ways to interact with a social object are illustrated in figure 48.

Figure 48: Different ways to interact with a social object

However, the relevant ways to interact with a social object depend both on the digital content and what the social object represents. For example, a social object can be a calendar event that represents a project meeting. A person might choose to *like* the calendar event, signaling to other people that he or she appreciates that the meeting will take place. By tagging the calendar event, it can be associated with other related social objects, for example a wiki page containing the meeting notes from the meeting. The wiki page with the meeting notes might be commented – have ancillary comments within and against the content.

When people interact with social objects, they also leave their digital fingerprints on the object. These fingerprints (or footprints) can tell us what they did, when they did it, which people they interacted with and in what context. They also help to reveal patterns of how work gets done, where certain information exists, who has a certain expertise, how information relates to other information, which people share common interest, who influences whom, and who is likely to answer certain kinds of questions. This metadata can then make it easier to find information, people, and expertise, and increase workspace awareness, both of which are important for effective and efficient collaboration and decision-making.

It is implied here that the digital work environment has been designed to be open and transparent, allowing anyone to participate and interact with anyone, and more or less anything, that is being shared (unless there are strong reasons for limiting access). This means that the person who *liked* the calendar event could just as well have been neither invited nor identified as a stakeholder to the project, but has become interested. It could be someone who works on a related subject and might have use for the output of the project, but who belongs to another organization and works at another location. The person might have noticed the project because he or she subscribed to the tag that was used – perhaps added by someone who was invited. Thus the meeting popped up on the person's digital 'radar screen'.

These kinds of serendipitous information discoveries, where you accidentally stumble upon something that opens new paths to success, are much more likely to happen in an open and transparent digital work environment than in one that is closed and opaque.

If people are to succeed in complex, dynamic, and unpredictable work environments, they need ways to discover and access information they didn't even know existed. If they mostly interact with the same people and do so in channels where no one can join your conversations unless invited, then the chances of gaining potentially relevant but unknown information are almost non-existing.

CREATING BETTER FILTERS

The explosion of digital content has made information abundant, not only on the Internet but also in the workplace. Many knowledge workers experience information overload. Enterprises struggle with managing the ever-increasing volumes of digital content. At the same time, there is a long tail of information needs that must be served if people are to create workspace awareness, to know when to contribute, and to make more well-informed decisions.

Paradoxically, serving the long tail of information needs will require sharing of much larger volumes of information. Social tools make this possible by making it easy for anyone to create and share digital content at almost no cost. Therefore, when putting social technology in the hands of people, there is a substantial risk that people will experience information overload when trying to make sense of every piece of information that is brought to their attention. The solution to this challenge isn't to hinder people from creating and sharing information, or to remove information they have already shared and that might be useful to someone at some point in time. It is to provide means for people to collectively organize the abundance of information and to create better filters that improve the signal-to-noise ratio.

Signal-to-noise ratio is a technical term that describes how much noise is in the output of a device in relation to the signal level. If there is too much noise, then people won't be able to receive the signal. Think about radio waves, or conversation in a crowded room. The term can also be used when talking about information relevancy and information overload, referring to the ratio of relevant and potentially useful information to irrelevant and useless information. If people are exposed to too much irrelevant information, they won't be able to find and make use of the information that is relevant and useful. So to improve the signal-to-noise ratio, we need better filters that make it easier for employees to find and discover relevant information. It isn't all about blocking out the noise, but about prioritising the signal.

First of all, a prerequisite for creating better filters is that we have access to good metadata that describes different aspects of a piece of digital content, such as its origin and what it is about. A lot of useful metadata can be created implicitly when people interact with the content.

Secondly, since social objects enable different ways to interact with digital content and capture data about these interactions, social objects help us create better filters. Systems can mine and analyze the captured data about how users interact with social objects and use that for recommending potentially relevant and useful digital content to users. A simple example is collaborative filtering; the system recommends digital content based on similar content that other users have interacted with.Collaborative filtering is common on e-commerce sites ("Other people who viewed this item also viewed these items"), but they can also be used for recommending digital content in a work context. For example, if you have shared a white paper about social technology with the colleagues you are connected to, the system might recommend that you take a look at other white papers or documents about social technology that colleagues have recently shared with their connections.

More powerful filters can be created when combining social objects with a person's *social graph*, the representation of the person's relationships with other people (figure 48). Social technology provides different ways for users to show people in their social networks what they think about a piece of information and if they vouch for it, for example by *liking* or marking it as a favorite. The system can then recommend digital content that one or more people in your social network found interesting or interacted with. The number of people can be an indicator of how valuable or important it is, but also whether it is relevant and useful to you. If several people you are connected to find the same piece of digital content interesting, it is likely you will too.

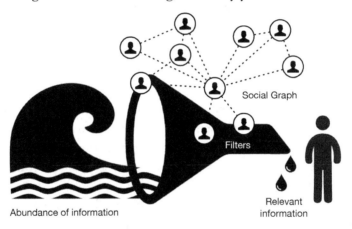

Figure 48: Social graph filtering

The amount of trust people have for a piece of information is also a factor that shouldn't be neglected or underestimated. If someone is to use certain information when making decisions, it is crucial that they trust it. If people they know and trust have recommended a piece of information, it is likely they will find the information more trustworthy than something no one with authority has vouched for.

There are many more ways that social technology can help reduce information overload and make it easier for employees to find and use information. For example, social technology makes it easy for users to access relevant information by following specific users, social objects, topics, groups, and so forth. Instead of having information pushed to them from someone who has decided what they should find relevant, they can choose for themselves what is relevant, or interesting. A lot of noise can be avoided this way. If people decide the information they receive from something they follow to be less relevant than expected, they can choose to unfollow.

INCREASING EMPLOYEE ENGAGEMENT

Although there are many factors that influence whether employees feel engaged at work, it has a lot to do with being seen, recognized, trusted, supported, and respected as both as professionals and human beings. It is important to have a caring and supportive work environment that empowers us to make the most of our talent and abilities as human beings. Our relationships with other employees matter a lot, not the least our relationships and trust in leaders and managers. Like any healthy relationship, the foundation is open, honest, and respectful communication.

Social technology makes it easier for people to communicate directly with each other and have rich, informal, and interactive communication on equal terms – even when they cannot meet face-to-face. This means that social technology can have a positive impact on employee engagement. Other ways that social technology could help increase employee engagement are listed in the table below.

What social technology can do	How it can help increase engagement
Connect new employees to the right people, information, teams, and communities when they join their new organization.	New employees can become integrated into the community and culture more quickly and find their social and professional identity within the organization.
Make employees' contributions visible and possible to recognize.	Knowing that their contributions are seen by managers and peers
Help employees with highly specialized roles in a distributed organization connect and interact with colleagues with similar roles or interests.	Employees will both feel less isolated and more valuable as they share their knowledge and expertise with like-minded people.
Increase workplace awareness so that employees know what is happening at work.	Reduces uncertainty and makes employees feel more confident and in control of their work situation.
Facilitate informal learning in the workplace through online sharing, conversations, and cooperation.	Better chance of personal and professional development.

SIZE MATTERS

Employees in small companies are more engaged than employees in larger companies. Much of this can likely be attributed to the fact that it is much easier to communicate and interact with people in a small company. It is also easier to be seen and make your voice heard, to get to know your colleagues, to have a direct communication with top management, to know what is happening at work, and so forth.

By connecting and bringing people together, creating social contexts online, and enabling rich, frequent, and spontaneous communication no matter the physical distance or organisation size, social technology can create a work environment that makes the company feel a lot smaller. It will help to increase employee engagement, because when it comes to employee engagement, smaller is better.

SOCIAL TECHNOLOGY IS NOT JUST A SET OF TOOLS

Most new technology products and solutions incorporate some social characteristics and are designed towards more openness, transparency, participation, conversation and recognition. These principles and the characteristics of social technology are now also used to transform existing IT systems in enterprises, such as ERP (Enterprise Resource Planning), CRM (Customer Relationship Management) systems, intranets and collaboration tools. The reason is often both to improve their social and collaborative capabilities and to make them more easy and attractive to use, designed to fit people's individual work styles instead of forcing people into a one-size-fits-all work style.

More and more software now include social technology. This might be a sign that the tide is turning and that organizations are shifting from technology-centric to people-centric thinking. Social technology will fundamentally have transformed the way we work, playing a central part in the digital transformation of enterprises. When all technology is being designed to fit with human nature and leverage human behavior and the desire and need to socialize with other people, we no longer need to call it social technology.

Successful digital transformation requires effective use of social technology because business has *always* been social. But until recently it was not possible to overcome the physical barriers to communication and interaction, at least not in a way that allowed people to communicate even about seemingly trivial things. When people make jokes about how some people share what they had for breakfast, they might not reflect on how fantastic it is that this is possible. Nowadays, people can share anything they like at almost no effort and cost, immediately and with global reach. They can start a conversation with anyone and almost any number of people. They can communicate directly with people regardless of where they are, or what position and status they have. This revolution in communication is now finding its way into organizations and enterprises, transforming how work is being done.

CHAPTER 13

DESIGNING THE COLLABORATIVE ORGANIZATION

"I believe that only those companies
that build collaboration into their DNA
by tapping into the collective expertise of all employees
– instead of just a few select leaders at the top –
will succeed,
as more and more market transitions occur at once."

John T. Chambers
Chairman of the Board and CEO of Cisco Systems

Imagine that you are dealing with a burning problem you don't know how to solve. You might be on to a solution, but you are not confident enough it will work to invest your time and energy in exploring it further. Besides, you are uncertain you have found your problem's root cause. You might just be missing some piece of information to understand the problem correctly.

So what do you do? The obvious thing would be to ask someone for help. But in many environments or situations, asking for help – and being able to receive it – is not as easy as it first might sound. The reasons why it is difficult may vary, but often it is difficult due to any or all of these reasons:

- You don't know whom to ask, because you don't know what skill, knowledge, or information is needed.
- You might not know enough people you can ask.
- You might not want to disturb those that you know, especially if you are not sure whether they can help you.

Say that all the above is true in this case. You have to find the expertise or information needed without knowing what kind of expertise, information, or person to look for, and you need it fast. Still, you don't want to waste the time and energy of the people within your personal network. So, you quickly evaluate the options you have left. Either you email your question to everyone in the organization, or your group, or you request to get your question published on the intranet.

The first option, to email your request for help to everyone is out of the question. Your email would likely be irrelevant and be seen as occupational spam by most people. Your personal reputation might be at risk, especially since you cannot describe what you are looking for in a clear and precise way. Besides, there is often no way to email everybody except by adding each person in the corporate address book as recipients. The ability to send 'all employee' emails is often restricted to top-level executives and the communication department.

Asking the intranet team to publish your question on the intranet is also not something to consider. It's just not that important and universally relevant for the home page. Besides, the intranet is primarily a platform for one-way communication and the chance that someone would click on your email address and send you a mail is likely low. Although there is an intranet area reserved for news and information related to your own department, it would not help you much to publish it there since the expertise you are looking for might be anywhere.

So, you go back to the drawing board again. Depending on what kind of person you are and the nature and urgency of your problem, you probably either continue to work on analyzing and solving the problem on your own, or you make the effort to send some emails, make some phone calls, and approach people you know to ask for help. This likely means they will need to forward your request for help to their own personal networks and coordinate any responses they get.

Now imagine that you have access to an open platform where the following is possible:

- You can post your request for help without spamming colleagues who are not interested in your problem.
- You can reach everyone in your organization.
- You need not know who might be able to help you in advance.
- You are not limited to the strength and size of your own personal network.
- You can involve many people, with any kind of skill or knowledge, from anywhere, without having to know any of them beforehand.

You might end up getting helped by an engineer in China who you've never met, a marketer who works at your office but whom you have never spoken with because you think she only does marketing, two interns who are writing their master thesis on a subject relating to your problem, and a colleague you already know but who you didn't consider asking because he's busy with a big project. Yet, they all think helping you will be worthwhile.

Who will help you, what position they have, what language they speak, or where they are located is of minor concern, if any at all. What is important is that they want to, and believe they can, help you, and that both of you share a platform that allows your request to reach them. The platform makes it as easy as possible for them to help you. That's the essence of social collaboration.

DEFINING SOCIAL COLLABORATION

Social collaboration is quite different from much of the traditional team-oriented collaboration we are used to. Social collaboration is about collaboration in a broader sense. It is about people collaborating as an enterprise and contributing to a shared purpose by directly and indirectly helping each other achieve goals. Whether we are having a conversation that clarifies a certain issue on a blog, updating information on a community wiki, or answering a question on a micro-blogging platform, we are in fact collaborating. Although this kind of collaboration is often indirect and subtle, our contributions can help individuals, teams, or the entire enterprise deal with major challenges.

Social collaboration extends beyond teams and might involve, directly or indirectly, anyone and any number of people. It also relies on using our personal networks to find people and information, as well as to rapidly diffuse, access, and filter relevant information, ideas, and expertise.

MAKING COLLABORATION HAPPEN NATURALLY

The physical distance between people reduces the likelihood they will collaborate. This is where social technology and the concept of social collaboration come into the picture.

To break the curse of physical proximity we must create virtual proximity. By using digital communication technology, we can increase the level of emotional closeness between people. We can make it *feel* like people on the other side of the world are sitting right next to you.

Figure 49: Social collaboration supports the five lower layers of the collaboration pyramid

Social technology allows people to perform the activities in the lower layers of the collaboration pyramid online, across communication barriers such as organizational groups and locations (figure 49). By making it easy to discover each other, leading us to serendipitous encounters, we can have spontaneous and informal conversations with each other, no matter where we are located or if we know each other or not. This way, communication and collaboration can happen naturally across groups and locations. People are no longer constrained by their organizational membership or the physical location where they work. They can be social anywhere, with anyone.

Online communities play an important role in making collaboration happen across groups and locations, as they connect people that share similar interests and goals, no matter their locations. Social technology also makes it possible to scale communication and collaboration far beyond the limits of the traditional team. It means that a company can build a company-wide community around a shared vision and shared goals. This has the potential not only to fuel innovation and collaboration across a large or dispersed workforce, but to overcome the communication barriers that lead to silo-thinking, which makes people put what is best for themselves or their team before what is best for the company.

IMPROVING THE EFFECTIVENESS OF COLLABORATION

Social collaboration plays an important role for the effectiveness of collaboration efforts. There are three factors that are especially important for the effectiveness of a collaboration effort; they are even more important when the work is highly inter-dependent. The inability to support these three factors is why many collaboration efforts in large and distributed organizations are ineffective, or fail entirely. Before discussing how social collaboration can help, let's look closer at the three factors.

HAVING THE RIGHT PEOPLE IN THE TEAM

The first factor, is to have the people with the right expertise and skills in the team. It's a rather obvious requirement, yet it can be hard to find and mobilize the right people in a large organization, and it is often the responsibility of management to do this. But management can't possibly know all the people in a large organization, and resource management systems are usually blunt tools for finding the right people to engage in a collaborative effort.

ACCESSING EXTERNAL INFORMATION

The second factor is about how easy it is to get access to external information; information that the group or team doesn't possess or have access to, or might be unaware of. In a complex, changing work environment where there are lots of interdependencies, having access to such information might be crucial if the team is to make the right decisions and avoid sub-optimization, rework, delays. These, and other kinds of waste, ultimately hurt the customer experience.

ACCESSING EXTERNAL EXPERTISE

The third factor is about having easy access to external expertise, people that can help team members solve problems, perform tasks, or create something they are less able to do by themselves. Subject-matter experts can offer guidance, share historical *lessons learned*, or become hands-on and collaborate directly.

SOCIAL COLLABORATION TO THE RESCUE

Social technology can improve all of these factors since it enables people to discover and connect with people and information outside their own teams. It helps to bridge structural holes and to strengthen any weak ties that exist between groups so that new external information can be made available to a group. Social technology also allows people to quickly find talent, expertise, and available resources so they can self-organize into teams that span geography and organizations. If social technology is used for social collaboration within the workforce, the effectiveness of a team will most likely increase due to the improved ability to find the right people for the team as well as better capabilities for team members to access relevant external information and expertise.

SUPPORTING NON-ROUTINE COLLABORATIVE WORK

Social collaboration is particularly valuable for non-routine and collaborative knowledge work – work that often requires both direct and indirect participation of many people to achieve the intended purpose or goals. In those situations, it's essential we can find and communicate with anyone – even people we don't (yet) know – and that they can participate and contribute.

There has been a lack of technology supporting non-routine and collaborative knowledge work. Most organizations have digital technology that support people working in highly structured and repeatable processes such as production, distribution, and sales. And there is groupware, or team collaboration tools, that support the semi-structured and semi-repeatable work that is often done in projects. But there is a big gap when it comes to supporting work that is barely repeatable, has no pre-defined structure, and is highly interdependent. For this kind of work, people need tools that help them manage and coordinate their work together with other people, beyond their teams. They need tools to connect, to share knowledge, to build community and, ultimately, to get their work done, which is about creating value for the customers.

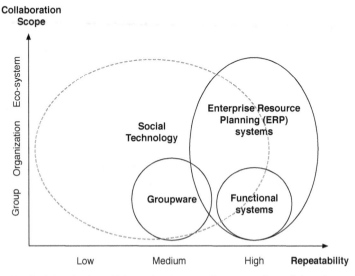

Figure 50: Social technology fill the technology gap for non-routine collaborative work

As illustrated in figure 50, social technology fills the technology gap that exists for non-routine and collaborative work. Many of the problems that occur in these kinds of situations can be addressed with social collaboration principles and technology by making it easy for people to have freeform many-to-many communication and interaction across time and space.

BREAKING THE TYRANNY OF EMAIL

Many organizations have allowed email to fill the technology gap discussed above, despite email not being suited for collaboration. The reason is, more often than not, a lack of viable alternatives to email, combined with the ingrained habits and culture among employees – using email for *all kinds* of communication.

As a result, inboxes are flooded by occupational spam, valuable information is locked into inboxes and left to die there, and the time people spend on organizing emails and trying to find information in their inboxes almost equals a part-time job. This is killing productivity, it is killing innovation, and it is killing employee engagement.

Social technology can solve many of the issues related to the overuse of email in organizations, and the enormous waste generated. It can unload much of the burden that is put on the recipient of an email. The inbox easily becomes a mess as emails about different things are mixed together. The emails are tied to the sender, not to a group or subjects. In addition, the recipient cannot choose what emails are relevant to receive and what emails are not. In an occupational spam culture, people carbon copy (CC) each other to keep colleagues informed. Living the mantra that it is better to be safe and sorry, they CC people on emails containing trivial information just to show that they are working. And whenever such an email turns into a 'reply all'-conversation, 'irrelevance hell' breaks loose.

As illustrated in figure 65, it falls to the recipient to sort out the mess this creates by organizing the emails. The alternative is to try living with the mess and working hard to find something of value in it.

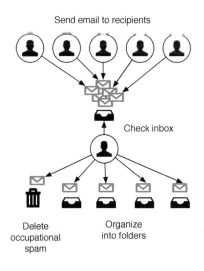

Figure 51: The burden is on the recipient to organize incoming emails

This situation can be contrasted with an 'opt-in' communication culture where each and everyone can choose what conversations they participate in and contribute to. This requires that the conversations happen on open platforms where people can see and discover ongoing conversations relevant to them. Instead of emailing the intended recipients, sometimes without knowing if they are interested in it or not, the sender posts the message to a group, blog, or project site. Tagging it with a subject allows people who are part of the group or interested in the subject to notice and read the message, either by actively checking for new messages or subscribing to new messages within an activity feed (figure 52).

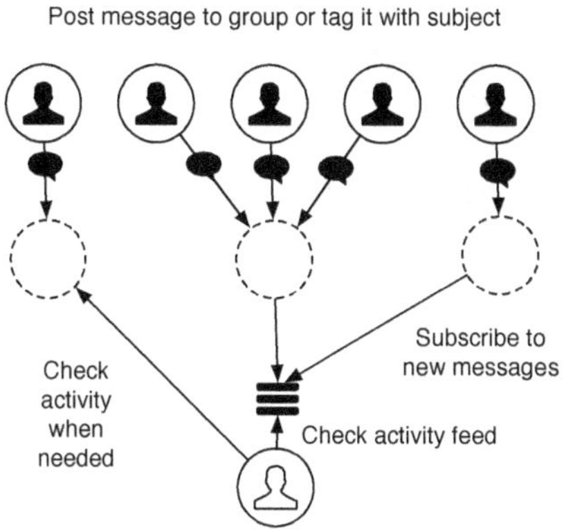

Figure 52: The sender organizes the information being communicated

This way, it is the senders that organize the communicated information. This means that the recipients don't have to, and thus huge amounts of waste can be eliminated. In addition, if someone wants to be informed about what is happening in, say, a team, it is the responsibility of that person to monitor the activity in the group. The person who posts a message doesn't need to put everyone they think *might* need to know about it on the list of CC recipients, and the people that would otherwise be on the list of CC recipients can avoid having their inboxes flooded by emails containing irrelevant or trivial information.

One common characteristic of social technology is the ability fo users to opt-in and opt-out of conversations, and to pre-structure the communication by posting it to groups or tagging it on open platforms. For example, instead of communicating with your project team using email, you can communicate using a team blog. You impose structure on the communication by sending the information to a specific context where it gets associated to previously communicated information and becomes available to anyone who has access to the blog. The information will not be buried in people's inboxes; it need not be pushed to their inboxes if they don't want it. From an organizational point of view, information and knowledge that can be of use by other people within the organization is captured and made available. Not as a separate activity, but as a by-product of a communication process.

BRINGING THE POWER OF NETWORKING TO THE PEOPLE

Until recently it was primarily people with formal positions in the hierarchical organization, such as managers, that had the power to build and maintain strong personal social networks and become part of informal networks within an organization. Their positions allowed them to allocate the time and resources to build their networks within their organizations.

Social networking technology now offer anyone in the workforce to build stronger personal networks inside the organization. The power of networking is available to anyone who finds it in their interest to connect and share by providing open spaces for starting and joining conversations across any barrier, such as organization, location position. This power, previously only available to the 'business elite' comprising salespeople, managers, and experts, can now be used by all employees.

In the light of this, one should not be too surprised if resistance comes from those who are already well connected and who feel threatened by the idea of more people getting well connected. They look suspiciously at the new social networking technology emerging from the social web, talking about them as security threats and productivity drains. What they need to see is how these technology allow people to get access to the information needed to make better decisions, faster. It is a win-win for the individual and for the organization. Organizations that ignore this and continue to help only a small fraction of their workforce become well connected, will be outperformed by companies thato connect all of their people regardless of position, budget, or other pre-defined criteria.

CHAPTER 14

FINDING
THE SWEET SPOTS FOR
SOCIAL COLLABORATION

*"We are always looking for the applications
that help people really have water-cooler talk,
something that we thought was impossible in a global business."*

Sheila Jordan
Vice CTO, Cisco

For years, tech-savvy early adopters brought social tools, such as blogs, wikis and micro-blogging, into work. Eventually, organizations began to see the benefits of these tools and to deploy software platforms to bring such tools to all their employees. The inclusion of social tools in new versions of major enterprise software has made the decision to introduce them easier Consequently, the tools have often been deployed and introduced to the users *without a purpose* or plan for how they should be used. It is almost as if the enterprise-wide deployment of these tools has taken corporate decision-makers, as well as early adopters, by surprise. Now that they have the tools, few have any guidance as to how the tools should be used, or how to integrate the tools into the daily work.

The lesson has been learned many times before when rolling-out new technology: find the problem to solve before you introduce a solution.

The primary problem social technology can address is to help people communicate and collaborate across organizational and geographical barriers. Social technology can also increase efficiency around process and task execution. For example, there can be extreme differences in efficiency between a scenario where you co-author content by emailing documents back and forth, and a scenario where you can co-author the content within the *same* document file in real-time.

Tools do matter. But it is for *what* and *how* we use them that make them matter. A tool should increase your capability, otherwise it has no reason to exist.

IMPROVING CORE KNOWLEDGE WORK CAPABILITIES

A good starting point when aiming to improve knowledge worker productivity is to improve the basic capabilities needed to do creative and collaborative knowledge work, as defined in chapter eight.

Let's take a look at a few of these capabilities to see how they can be improved: becoming aware, creating information, sharing information, and locating expertise. For each capability, one or several examples of common practices, as well as new practices enabled by social technology, will be described.

BECOMING AWARE

Workspace awareness is critical for all collaborative work. If you don't know what your colleagues are doing or what they need and when, how can you possibly know how and when you should contribute to a joint effort?

Work in most organizations is becoming more interdependent and collaborative. It is also becoming more common to work with people from different locations, using digital communication tools. Compared to when we used to work with people in close proximity, it has become harder to build workplace awareness.

To increase our workspace awareness, digital work environments need to provide us with contextual information. As individuals, we need to share more of such information, not only with the people we work with, but also with anyone who could have interest in knowing what we are doing. We need to inform our colleagues about seemingly trivial things, such as where we are, what we are reading, and with whom we are interacting.

CURRENT PRACTICES

Most of us build workplace awareness by asking our colleagues what they are up to, either when meeting face-to-face or via a digital communication tool such as email. Instead of passively monitoring our physical work environment, we actively request information from each other. It consumes a lot of our time and energy and, by interrupting people, we also make colleagues less productive. Since much of the information we need to create workplace awareness is trivial, we often refrain from requesting it from our colleagues because it is not worth disturbing them.

It is relatively easy to ask colleagues we know, or who work in our close proximity, about their day and work. We are also more likely to have spontaneous and informal conversations with them that can bring us new information.

When we need to know what other teams at other locations, or people we don't know, are doing, asking becomes much harder. We have to know whom to contact and preferably have a relationship with that person to even bother to ask. We are also less likely to bump into such people and have those spontaneous and informal conversations.

If individuals and teams do not proactively and frequently share information about what they are doing, and if there is no way to discover and access it, the only information we will get is what we explicitly ask for. Given the time and energy we need to invest, and the barriers we will have to overcome, it won't be much information at all. It definitely won't be enough to build workplace awareness.

NEW PRACTICES

In the New York Times article, 'Brave New World of Digital Intimacy', from 2008, Clive Thompson made the concept of ambient awareness, which has been used by social scientists, available to a wider audience. He used the news feed in Facebook as an example of an environment that creates ambient awareness:

> *"Each little update — each individual bit of social information — is insignificant on its own, even supremely mundane. But taken together, over time, the little snippets coalesce into a surprisingly sophisticated portrait of your friends' and family members' lives, like thousands of dots making a pointillist painting."*

Thompson described the news feed as something that "… brings back the dynamics of small-town life, where everybody knows your business". According to Thompson, Facebook founder Mark Zuckerberg attributed the introduction of the news feed feature, providing Facebook users with constant, up-to-the-minute updates on what other people they know are up to, as central to Facebook's success.

It shouldn't be very hard to see the use case for the equivalent of the Facebook news feed inside a large organization. If people work out loud, actively sharing small updates on what they are doing, other people can choose to subscribe to their updates. By passively monitoring friends' feeds, they can become aware of what other people and teams are doing without investing much time or energy. They will build the workplace awareness that tells them when, why, and how to act in collaborative work contexts.

CO-CREATING

When separated by space or time, we often communicate with each other by creating information in the form of various types of digital content, such as text and graphics. As illustrated in figure 66 below, this is referred to as asynchronous communication, meaning that people communicate indirectly with each other through some digital content. It allows communication even when separated by both time and space. In most organizations, this means that people create documents they make accessible to others via email, file shares, or collaboration software.

It has always been a challenge to create information in a way that allows for effective communication, and it is especially hard when you don't know in advance who will use the information. As knowledge work is becoming increasingly collaborative, creating information is often a collaborative effort that involves two or more people. Creating information with other people efficiently is always a challenging task, and even more so when people cannot meet face-to-face to do so but need to do it remotely using digital tools.

Creating with others is also something that builds community, culture (shared attitudes and behaviors), and social identity (our identity in relationship to the community). In a work environment where people don't get to meet everyone they work with on a daily basis, these aspects of co-creation become increasingly important if people are to be engaged and productive.

There are, in other words, many reasons why it should be as easy to co-create digital information as possible.

COMMON PRACTICES

The communication in most organizations is still document-centric and depends on email for exchanging information. The information exchanged is predominantly represented as text in documents. The use of other types of content such as graphics and video is usually limited.

When exchanging documents via email. The document – and thus the information in it – is duplicated for each recipient. This makes the co-creation process messy and erroneous, especially when we consider version control and review processes.

Take the process of creating a project definition as an example. It often begins with the project manager creating a project definition outline in a document. The content is heavy on text but might include a few graphics. To allow other team members to contribute to the project definition, the document is sent via email as an attachment to the project team members so they can review it and suggest updates.

The team members then make changes directly to the document and then send it back to the project manager as an attachment via email. The project manager incorporates any changes into his own local document. This process is likely repeated a few times. When the project definition is completed, the document is stored in a document library on a file server or team site on a collaboration platform. Other project stakeholders receive it via email as an attachment.

There are many problems with this way of working. For example, when people work on a document and exchange the document via email, a copy of the document is created for each and every recipient. This makes it a very cumbersome task to collect and manage any changes to the document since, in fact, people are working on *multiple* documents. Someone has to integrate the changes into a single document. When doing so, tracing who made a certain change becomes hard. There will also be a lot of emails sent back and forth, adding to the huge amount of email that most knowledge workers already struggle to cope with.

NEW PRACTICES

New consumer technology has made it cheaper and easier than ever to create or capture information and to use various types of content, such as text, video, graphics, and sound. This makes it possible to choose a type of content that allows more effective communication. And yes, sometimes a picture is worth a thousand words.

With social technology, anything that is created or captured with digital devices can be shared as social objects on social platforms, which allows for open and conversational co-creation processes involving many people. Potentially anyone can participate in the co-creation process, thereby enabling a diversity of ideas, experiences, and opinions to fuel the conversation and co-creation process.

As people interact with the same social objects (with the latest version always presented to everyone), there is no duplication of information and no versioning mess. In addition, the lack of pre-imposed structure and the possibility to use any type of content facilitates a more constructive and creative co-creation process. As a side effect, more open, interactive, and participatory co-creation processes will help to build community, culture, and social identity even if the workforce is spread across the world.

FINDING PEOPLE AND EXPERTISE

In the past, we relied solely on our personal networks and people in our close proximity for help. When seeking formally appointed experts we would have to hope our network could help, or try to identify experts via the hierarchical organizational chart.

Today, when dealing with increasingly complex tasks, it is more important than ever to quickly locate the expertise we need to get the work done. Yet, no formally appointed single expert can hold all the knowledge and expertise needed within a specific domain. The people who possess the knowledge or expertise we need might be located anywhere in the world.

If you want to solve a problem or find an answer to a question, it is often a better strategy to ask a colleague for help, rather than try to find and interpret the information encoded in some form of content. The ability to quickly find the right person to talk to is therefore often more important than finding relevant content. Yet to do so can be a daunting or almost impossible task within a large organization, where you might not know who possesses the knowledge or expertise you need.

CURRENT PRACTICES

The most common way to locate expertise is to search for a specific person in an employee directory. That is, if you're lucky to have one single employee directory; if not, you will need to search in multiple directories.

Finding people by how they are described in a database can work quite well if you know exactly what you are looking for and if people have expressed their expertise in the same terminology. The search engine might help you in the matching process by adding some intelligence, such as ranking and guided search. But active searching is often a blunt tool. Too often, people haven't accurately described their expertise, or they have used different descriptors than you might expect, or even know to use in your search.

If searching doesn't help, the next thing you might do is to ask people you know, using email, phone, or face-to-face conversations if they know someone who has the expertise you need. It will help if you have a large and broad network that stretches throughout the enterprise. But each one of your contacts will need to invest some time and energy in considering and perhaps distributing your query to their contacts and to report any answers back to you. All in all, the process will be time-consuming and the lead times will be long.

NEW PRACTICES

If, instead, you used an enterprise social networking platform, then you could describe what you need in a message, and tag it with relevant synonyms (relating to the topic and how other people might describe the expertise you seek). Anyone who has access to the platform and can and wants to reply to your message can do so.

If you have tagged your question with relevant keywords, then people that follow one or more of those tags might see your message in their activity feed. Tags help you reach people outside of your personal network. To assist in tagging, the system usually suggests commonly used tags as you type. Perhaps there is a community related to the tags you use, so the system might notify you about it. If so, you can choose to post the question directly to the community.

If anyone that happen to see your message has the expertise you seek, they could reply to your message. They can also forward your message into *their* social networks simply by interacting with it, such as *liking* it. The number of people that might see your message is multiplied with the number of contacts that each person has in their social networks.

Asking for help is often much more effective than searching for information. According to a study by British car insurance company, Sheila's Wheels, the old stereotype that most men are less likely than women to ask for directions seems to be true. More than 26 percent of the men waited at least an hour before asking for directions; 12 percent were too stubborn to ask at all. As a result, the study suggest, the average male drives an extra 276 miles every year – compared to 256 miles for women.[1] Regardless of the gender differences, a lot of waste could be avoided if people were more willing to ask other people for information.

There's another thing about asking questions to many people at the same time. Instead of finding *the* expert, you can end up with multiple answers that together could provide better guidance than if you had asked a single expert. The people who answer your question might have something unique to contribute or, when they see others' contributions, develop and share new insights within the conversation.

IMPROVING EASILY REPEATABLE PROCESSES

When it comes to collaborative non-routine knowledge work, it makes more sense to strengthen the *capabilities* that enable knowledge workers to efficiently perform tasks than to focus on the specific *processes*. It is a better strategy to give them the means to organize and manage their work, and to make it easy for them to move from one activity to another.

It is a slightly different story for more structured and repeatable processes. By applying social design principles and technology that enable more effective communication and collaboration, processes that span across organizational groups and locations can be improved. Exactly what improvement opportunities might exist depends on the specific process and business context, but some common areas of improvement are illustrated in figure 53.

---

1 Men lost for longer, http://www.sheilaswheels.com/media/MEN_LOST_FOR_LONGER.html

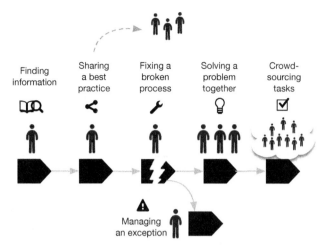

Figure 53: Typical improvement areas in easily repeatable processes

For example, social technology can enable the following improvement opportunities for a process:

- Handling exceptions and problems can be improved by greater ability to quickly mobilize and engage the right people and expertise.
- Simple routine tasks can be crowd-sourced internally, using a pool of available people, and speed up the process and optimizing the organization's resource usage.
- Efficiency can be improved by greater ability to share, find, and reuse existing knowledge
- New team members can be on-boarded and become fully productive faster.
- Best practices and continuous improvements can be shared more easily between different teams that work with the same process.

COMMUNICATION CHALLENGES IN PROCESSES

Many processes span multiple organizational groups and locations, and an enterprise often involves multiple organizations. Thus, people from different groups from the same and different organisations need to collaborate to improve performance across the complete value chain.

Besides organizational and geographical barriers, there might be barriers such as different systems and tools, time zones, cultures, and languages. Teamwork across such barriers is hard and often comes unnaturally to people. They find it more natural to work with people in their own team, who they know and who share the same kinds of tasks and goals. As a result, process improvements are typically made locally within an organizational group, such as Marketing or R&D, often at the expense of improvements to the whole process which might cut across several organizational groups. The group often fails to see the big picture and also the dependencies for other groups. Thus, local optimization efforts might have negative consequences for other groups and lead to sub-optimization for the enterprise as a whole.

To improve a process that spans multiple locations and organizations, the big picture needs to be clear to all involved: the customer, their needs, the expected output and outcome, who else participates, and the flow of activities. Those involved also need to communicate and collaborate easily with other teams, so that they can share problems and improvement ideas, decide which solutions to implement, and then design and implement the changes together. It requires true enterprise-wide involvement where collaboration happens naturally, not only within teams but also across organizations and locations. This in turn requires effective use of social technology so that rich, spontaneous, and frequent digital communication and interaction, can happen at almost no cost.

HOW TO IMPROVE A PROCESS

There is a straightforward way to identify improvement opportunities for an easily repeatable process or activity and it involves using framework with knowledge work capabilities from chapter 9 and the five principles from chapter 11:

- Identify required capabilities and their place in the process.
- Explore how capabilities can be improved by applying the five principles of collaborative communication.

Let's take sales lead generation as an example. Identifying sales leads is the first step of a sales process and it is often the responsibility of the marketing or sales organization. The purpose is to capture a sales lead that might be converted to a sale. If we assume that the conversion rate remains the same as more sales leads are captured, more sales leads will generate more sales. But this can be hard to achieve. The marketing and sales organization has limited resources and might already be using those resources in a near optimal way. There doesn't seem to be much room for improvement when it comes to capturing more sales leads.

What if not just sales people, but anyone who works for a company might be exposed to sales opportunities? For example, a field technician might identify a sales opportunity while visiting a customer site to service installed equipment. Or a consultant might identify a sales opportunity when talking to another parent when picking up his kids at childcare. What if they could capture and share sales leads that can be funneled into the sales process? They don't work within the marketing or sales organization, but why should that stop them from participating in the sales process?

If a company decides it wants to engage every employee in lead generation, there are two capabilities that are relevant:

- **Share information:** Anyone needs to be able to capture and share sales leads.
- **Become aware:** The sales people need to become aware of potential sale signals so they can act upon them and convert them to sales.

When these capabilities have been identified and assessed, the company can explore how the capability can be improved to better support sales generation activity within the sales process. This can be by applying the five principles of collaborative communication (chapter ten) as described below.

Participation: This is the principle we have already applied when identifying the improvement opportunity. It allows anyone to participate in the sales process. For example, a service technician observes a customer need while visiting a customer site and decides to participate in the sales process by capturing and sharing a sales lead.

Openness: If the sales lead is shared openly, it means that potentially anyone within the company could find or discover it. Not only is it brought to the attention of the responsible sales person. Other colleagues who might have relevant information or knowledge about the customer can discover the sales lead and share what they know. Or it might make someone think of other customers that have the same need, generating even more sales leads.

Transparency: If it is easy to trace the sales lead to the person who shared it, it is possible to request more information from that person. The time and location might also be relevant to know.

Conversation: If those now involved can have a conversation about the sales lead, the responsible sales person can quickly get a better understanding of the customer's need by having a two-way conversation.

Recognition: If the service technician who captured and shared the sales lead is recognized, it will motivate him to continue capturing and sharing lead signals. If he is recognized in public, it might also encourage others to follow his example.

With social technology, the sales process can be redesigned to leverage collective human behaviors in the way described in the example above. The business impact of such a redesign will be that more sales leads are generated. Sales are likely to increase not only because there are more leads to convert into sales, but also because more information can be obtained about the customer's need, and thus make it easier to convert a lead into a sale. The sales people get more leads to follow and tools to get a better understanding of the needs of potentially new or existing customers.

CHAPTER 15

MAKING CHANGE HAPPEN

*"The largest enemy of change and leadership isn't a 'no'.
It's a 'not yet'.
'Not yet' is the safest, easiest way to forestall change.
'Not yet' gives the status quo a chance to regroup
and put off the inevitable for just a little while longer.
Change almost never fails because it's too early.
It almost always fails because it's too late."*

*Seth Godin
American author, entrepreneur, marketer, and public speaker*

We must not forget that technology is just one part of the equation. Change is 90 percent about people and 10 percent about technology. The technology is the easy part. The really hard part is to change people's attitudes and behaviors. Most people will cling to their existing behaviors and practices. An existing behavior that has been automated and turned into a habit requires a lot of effort to change, even if the new behavior will make things better. People often stick to inefficient behaviors simply because they have automated them – they do them on autopilot. If the system doesn't force or encourage them to change their habits, then why should they?

Even harder to change than habits is the communication culture: the norms that tell us how, what, and with whom we should communicate. And that is exactly what a company needs to change if it is to realize the potential benefits of social technology. It is not enough to change the tools; we need to change the system. All relevant components that make up the system must all be modified to support the change we want: goals and measures, leadership and management practices, processes and routines, incentive systems, policies and rules, IT systems.

So, how do we make change happen?

THE CHALLENGE OF BREAKING HABITS

Change is hard. Once we have learned how to do something a certain way, it becomes a habit. It takes serious effort to reprogram ourselves to behave and do something in a different way. And even if we are willing to make the effort to change, our environment often reinforces our existing habits. To change, we need other people to change as well.

It is hard to change the way we do routine work, but it is even harder to change how we do non-routine work. Routine work is often encoded in our IT systems. We can change it by changing the systems. But changing how we do non-routine work, such as problem solving, is an entirely different thing. We need to change the way we think.

Change also takes time. When email was introduced in organizations, it took many years to figure out the business use cases and to achieve widespread adoption. Organizations stumbled at the same barriers to adoption that are now hindering them to adopt social technology, especially those that have to do with people changing their mindsets and habits.

WHY SOCIAL TECHNOLOGY INITIATIVES FAIL

One might assume that social technology is easier for people to adopt because the technology itself fits and leverages human behaviors. Yet a lot of organizations have failed miserably when deploying social technology, such as enterprise social networking platforms. After an initial spike in adoption, the usage rate often falls. Soon the platform turns into a ghost town. There are two main reasons why this happens.

First of all, people often consider new tools for non-routine work as optional to adopt and use. If they don't want to use them, or they don't see why they should make an effort to change how they work, they can always stick to their existing tools and habits. Such as using email and attachments for co-creating information. This in stark contrast to when a new tool or system is being introduced for an easily repeatable process. Take ERP (Enterprise Resource Planning) systems as an example. An ERP system dictates both the process and how individual tasks should be performed. Whenever an ERP system is replaced, it means the processes and tasks are replaced. Everyone who is participating in the affected processes must adopt the new system and hence also the new ways of working that comes with it. If they don't, they can just as well quit their jobs.

Secondly, most organizations underestimate the kind and magnitude of the change that social technology brings. Social technology doesn't just change how people work, such as how they perform a task; social technology enables people to communicate in new ways. Therefore, when it is truly adopted by an organization, it changes the communication culture of an organization.

The communication culture is the shared attitudes and behaviors that determine how and with whom we communicate, including what tools we use for communication. It also determines what we communicate and the ways we perceive and describe ourselves to others, such as our roles, responsibilities, expertise, and interests. Culture touches on people's true values and deeply entrenched attitudes. Obviously, it is much harder to change people's values and attitudes than how people work. If the communication culture isn't changed as a result of introducing a social tool, it means people will eventually abandon it. Or they will use it in the same way they used their old tools, paving cow paths.

Changing the communication culture of an organization usually takes a long time. Just think about how long it took for email, first introduced in organizations in the late '70s and early '80s, to become fully adopted. It also turned out that email fundamentally change how people communicated in organizations.

THE TRUE SIGNS OF CHANGE

So how does one know if the communication culture is changing or not? Well, it is clearly not enough to measure how many people are using a new communication tool.

Once a critical mass of people within the organisation have adopted an open communication tool, we need to look for changes in how people communicate and perceive themselves. For example, formally appointed experts may start to perceive and describe themselves more as mentors and connectors than as experts or gurus. This is because, in practice, they use social technology, such as an enterprise social networking platform, to guide their colleagues in how to find information and to put them in direct contact with people in their own networks.

Another example is when customer service people perceive and describe themselves more as sales representatives and idea generators. This is likely to happen when they use social technology to capture and share sales opportunities and ideas on how to improve the customer experience, based on their conversations and interaction with customers.

PUTTING PEOPLE AND CULTURE FIRST

Gartner (2013) recently predicted 80 percent of all internal social business efforts will fail, largely due to the way organizations approach them. A sure path to failure is the technology-focused way that most organizations still use when defining and implementing IT systems.

Technology-focus turns any deployed social technology into yet another IT silo, disconnected and isolated from daily work in terms of tasks and processes that people do. This is a paradox, since the real business value of implementing social technology comes when its goal is to improve communication and collaboration across organizational, geographical, and IT system silos.

Organizations that focus too much on technology also fail to take the needs of the users as their starting point. They invest primarily in the tools or platforms deployed and much less in facilitating adoption and change. This results in low adoption and low ROI. No sustained change to ways of working or the communication culture is possible with such a narrow focus.

While technology can be an enabler and accelerator of change, change is always about people and culture. To succeed with a transformation, an organization must first seek to understand the people, the nature of the work they do, and the situations they find themselves in.

Social technology changes how we communicate and interact with each other. When we use such technology to communicate, interact, and collaborate with each other, we show our behaviors through our actions. Social technology makes our actions become visible to others. We might influence colleagues who might not share the same values or behaviors. And eventually they might adopt similar behaviors and even come to value more open ways of communicating and working (see figure 54).

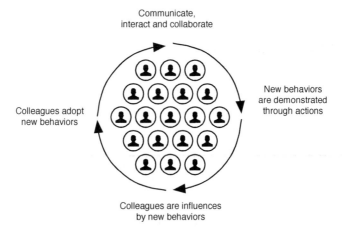

Figure 54: The communication culture is shaped by our ongoing communication and interaction

In this way, the technology can become a platform for bringing about a new and more collaborative communication culture within an organization. But there must always be a spark somewhere that starts this change, and that spark can only come from people. Social technology can empower people to work smarter together, to climb the collaboration pyramid, and collaborate naturally across organizational and geographical silos. But it will not happen unless the formal and informal leaders within the organization adopt social technology and actively work to change the communication culture of their organization – embracing the principles of openness, transparency, participation, dialog, and recognition.

REFERENCES

2012 Adoption Insight report. (2012). Retrieved from: http://www.ltc4.org/Resources/Documents/Neochange%202012%20Adoption%20Insight%20Report_v2.pdf

2013 Federal Employee Viewpoint Survey Results. (2013). United Stats Office of Personnel Management. Rerrived from: http://www.fedview.opm.gov/2013files/2013_Governmentwide_Management_Report.PDF

Albanesi, S., Gregory, V., Patterson, C. & Şahin, A. (2013). *Is Job Polarization Holding Back the Labor Market?.* Liberty Street Economics blog. Retrieved from: http://libertystreeteconomics.newyorkfed.org/2013/03/is-job-polarization-holding-back-the-labor-market.html

Allen, T. J. (1977). *Managing the Flow of Technology.* Cambridge, Massachusetts, and London, England. The MIT Press.

Aral, S., Brynjolfsson, E. & Van Alstyne, M.W. (2007). *Productivity Effects of Information Diffusion in Networks.* Retrieved from: http://papers.ssrn.com/sol3/papers.cfm?abstract_id=987499

Bates, M. (2003). *Towards An Integrated Model of Information Seeking and Searching.* University of California, Los Angeles. Retrieved from: http://pages.gseis.ucla.edu/faculty/bates/articles/info_SeekSearch-i-030329.html

Beardsley, S.C, Johnson, B.C. & Manyika, J.M. (2006). *Competitive advantage from better interactions.* The McKinsey Quarterly. Retrieved from: http://www.executivesondemand.net/managementsourcing/images/stories/artigos_pdf/produtividade/Competitive_advantage_from_better_interactions.pdf

Bennett, D. (2013). *The Dunbar Number, From the Guru of Social Networks.* Bloomberg Business. Retrieved from: http://www.bloomberg.com/bw/articles/2013-01-10/the-dunbar-number-from-the-guru-of-social-networks#p2

Birkinshaw, J. and Cohen, J. (2013). *Make Time for the Work That Matters.* Harvard Business Review. Retrieved from: http://hbr.org/2013/09/make-time-for-the-work-that-matters/ar/1

Blau, M. (2010). *The Internet as a new way of life.* Psychotherapy Networker. Retrieved from: https://www.psychotherapynetworker.org/magazine/recentissues/2010-septoct/item/1094-the-relationship-revolution

Brand, S., Kelly, K. & Dyson, G. (2011). *The Third Culture*. Edge 338. Retrieved from: http://www.edge.org/documents/archive/edge338.html

Brinkley, I., Fauth, R., Mahdon, M. & Theodoropoulou, S. (2009). *Knowledge Workers and Knowledge Work - A Knowledge Economy Programme Report*. The Work Foundation. Retrieved from: http://www.theworkfoundation.com/assets/docs/publications/213_know_work_survey170309.pdf

Bryan, L.L., Matson, E. & Weiss, L. M. (2007). *Harnessing the power of informal employee networks*. The McKinsey Quarterly. Retrieved from: http://www.mckinsey.com/insights/organization/harnessing_the_power_of_informal_employee_networks

Buczek, L. (2009). *Why Intel is investing in Social Computing*. IT Peer Network, Intel. Retrieved from: https://communities.intel.com/community/itpeernetwork/blog/authors/LaurieBuczek

Buczek, L. & Harkins, M. (2009). *Developing an Enterprise Social Computing Strategy. Intel Corporation*. Retrieved from: http://download.intel.com/it/pdf/Developing_an_Enterprise_Social_Computing_strategy.pdf

Chew, J. (2012). *Fortune 500 Extinction*. csinvesting. Retrieved from: http://csinvesting.org/tag/corporate-extinction/

Chui, M., Manyika, J., Bughin, J., Dobbs, R., Roxburgh, C., Sarrazin, H., Sands, G. & Westergren, M. (2012). *The social economy: Unlocking value and productivity through social technologies*. Retrieved from: http://www.mckinsey.com/insights/high_tech_telecoms_internet/the_social_economy

Chui, M., Miller, A.m & Roberts, R.P. (2009). *Six Ways to make Web 2.0 work*. The McKinsey Quarterly. Retrieved from: http://www.mckinseyquarterly.com/Six_ways_to_make_Web_20_work_2294

Cohen, J. (2010). *Getting Rid of the Busy Work so You Can Get to Work. Management Innovation Exchange*. Retrieved from: http://www.managementexchange.com/story/getting-rid-busy-work-so-you-can-get-work

Cohen, J. and Birkinshaw, J. (2013). *Make Your Knowledge Workers More Productive*. Harvard Business Review. Retrieved from: http://blogs.hbr.org/2013/09/make-your-knowledge-workers-more-productive/

Crabtree, S. (2013). *Worldwide, 13% of Employees Are Engaged at Work*. Gallup. Retrieved from: http://www.gallup.com/poll/165269/

worldwide-employees-engaged-work.aspx

Data Warehousing Special Report. (2002). The Data Warehousing Institute (TDWI).

Daily, B. (2014). *Winning on the Field: The Critical Role of Managers in Driving Engagement Via Diversity & Inclusion.* RoundPegg. Retrieved from: http://sto.ly/w6nV

Denning, D.E. (1990). Concerning Hackers Who Break into Computer Systems. *Proceedings of the 13th National Computer Security Conference*, pp. 653-664. Retrieved from: http://www.cs.georgetown. edu/~denning/hackers/Hackers-NCSC.txt

Drucker, P. F. (1959). *Landmarks of Tomorrow.* New York: Harper.

Dunbar's number. (2015). Wikipedia, the free encyclopedia. Retrieved from: http://en.wikipedia.org/wiki/Dunbar's_number

Economies of Scale: The Long Run – Increases in Scale. (2014). Economies Online. Retrieved from: http://www.economicsonline.co.uk/Business_economics/Economies_of_scale.html

Employee Engagement. (2015). Wikipedia, the free encyclopedia. Retrieved from: http://en.wikipedia.org/wiki/Employee_engagement

Engelhardt, A. (2006). *The 3/2 Rule Revisited.* Cybaea. Retrieved from: http://www.cybaea.net/Blogs/employee_productivity_sector.html

Feldman, S. & Sherman, C. (2001). *The High Cost of Not Finding Information.* IDC. Retrieved from: http://www.ejitime.com/materials/IDC%20on%20The%20High%20Cost%20Of%20Not%20Finding%20Information.pdf

Finley, K. (2011). *Was Eric Schmidt Wrong About the Historical Scale of the Internet?*. readwrite. Retrieved from: http://readwrite.com/2011/02/07/are-we-really-creating-as-much

Gallo, C. (2007). *Body Language: A Key to Success in the Workplace.* Yahoo Finance. Retrieved from http://finance.yahoo.com/news/pf_article_102425.html.

Gladwell, M. (2002). *The Tipping Point: How Little Things Can Make a Big Difference.* Back Bay Books.

Gleick, J. (2011). *The Information*. Pantheon Books.

Godin, S. (2008). *Tribes: We need you to lead us*. Portfolio.

Gonzalez-Rivas, G. & Larsson, L. (2010). *Far from the Factory: Lean for the Information Age*. Productivity Press.

Hartung, A. (2015). *Bigger Is Not Always Better - Why Amazon Is Worth More Than Walmart*. Forbes. Retrieved from: http://www.forbes.com/sites/adamhartung/2015/07/25/bigger-is-not-always-better-why-amazon-is-worth-more-than-walmart/2/

Hierarchic Control System. (2015). Wikipedia, the free encyclopedia. Retrieved from: http://en.wikipedia.org/wiki/Hierarchical_control_system

Impact of employee engagement on productivity. (2012). Insync Surveys. Retrieved from: http://www.insyncsurveys.com.au/resources/articles/employee-engagement/2012/10/impact-of-employee-engagement-on-productivity/

Information asymmetry. (2015). Wikipedia, the free encyclopedia. Retrieved from: http://en.wikipedia.org/wiki/Information_asymmetry

Intuit 2020 Research Report - Twenty Trends That Will Shape The Next Decade. (2010) Intuit. Retrieved from: http://about.intuit.com/futureofsmallbusiness/

Kiesler, S. and J. N. Cummings. (2002). *What Do We Know about Proximity and Distance in Work Groups? A Legacy of Research*. In *Distributed Work*. P. J. Hinds and S. Kiesler. Cambridge, Massachusetts, The MIT Press.

Kolsky, E. (2010). *What is an Experience Continuum (and how do I get one)?*. mycustomer.com. Retrieved from: http://www.mycustomer.com/topic/customer-experience/esteban-kolsky-what-experience-continuum-and-how-do-i-get-one/109258

Kotter, J.P. (2011). *Hierarchy and Network: Two Structures, One Organization*. Harvard Business Review. Retrieved from: http://blogs.hbr.org/kotter/2011/05/two-structures-one-organizatio.html

Kossek, E.E., Hammer, L.B, Thompson, R.J. & Burke, L.B. (2014).

Leveraging Workplace Flexibility for Engagement and Productivity. Retrieved from http://www.shrm.org/about/foundation/products/documents/9-14%20work-flex%20epg-final.pdf

Kouzes, J.M. (2000). *Link Me to Your Leader.* Business 2.0.

Locke. C., Searls, D., Weinberger, D. & Levine, R. (2000). *The Cluetrain Manifesto.* New York. Basic Books

Lovejoy. B. (2014). *iPhone 6 production by the numbers: 100 production lines, 200k workers, 540k phones a day.* 9to5Mac. Retrieved from: http://9to5mac.com/2014/09/17/iphone-6-production-by-the-numbers-100-production-lines-200k-workers-540k-phones-a-day/

Mancini, J. [John Mancini]. (2008). *State of the ECM Industry Survey* [Online presentation]. Retrieved from: http://www.slideshare.net/jmancini77/aiim-state-of-the-ecm-industry-survey

Mann, J., Austin, T., Drakos, N. Rozwell, C. & Walls, A. (2012). *Predicts 2013: Social and Collaboration Go Deeper and Wider.* Gartner. Retrieved from: http://www.gartner.com/resId=2254316

McLoughlin, A. (2011). *Back to the (Office of the) Future.* GigaOM. Retrieved from: https://gigaom.com/2011/04/01/back-to-the-office-of-the-future/

Melloy, J. (2015). *Dominant: Apple takes 90% of smartphone profits.* CNBC. Retrieved from: http://www.cnbc.com/2015/02/09/dominant-apple-takes-90-of-smartphone-profits.html

Men lost for longer. (2010). Sheilas Wheels. Retrieved from: http://www.sheilaswheels.com/media/MEN_LOST_FOR_LONGER.html

Morville, P. (2005). *Ambient Findability: What We Find Changes Who We Become.* O'Reilly Media.

Nearly half of UK office workers free to roam and work from home. (2013). Virgin Media Business. Retrieved from: http://www.virginmediabusiness.co.uk/News-and-events/News/News-archives/2013/Nearly-half-of-UK-office-workers-free-to-roam-and-work-from-home/

O'Reilly Media [O'Reilly]. (2008, September 19). *Web 2.0 Expo NY: Clay Shirky (shirky.com) It's Not Information Overload. It's Filter Failure* [Video file]. Retrieved from: http://www.youtube.com/watch?v=LabqeJEOQyI

Patel, S. (2011). *Why Exception Handling Should be the Rule*. Retrieved from: http://www.pretzellogic.org/2011/07/21/why-exception-handling-should-be-the-rule/

Pfeffer, J. & Sutton, R.I. (2000). The Knowing-Doing Gap: How Smart Companies Turn Knowledge into Action. Harvard Business School Press.

Pozen, R.C. (2011). *Managing Yourself: Extreme Productivity*. Harvard Business Review. Retrieved from: http://hbr.org/2011/05/managing-yourself-extreme-productivity/ar/1

Principle of least effort. (2015). Wikipedia, the free encyclopedia. Retrieved from: http://en.wikipedia.org/wiki/Principle_of_least_effort

Re-engaging with engagement. (2010). Economist Intelligence Unit. Retrieved from: http://www.economistinsights.com/sites/default/files/LON%20-%20PL%20-%20Hay%20report_WEB.pdf

Rinde, S. (2007). *SAP Influencer Summit #3 – SAP missing the biggest opportunity ever?*. Retrieved from: http://thingamy.typepad.com/sigs_blog/2007/12/sap-influence-2.html

Riverhead Books [RiverheadBooks]. (2010, September 17). *Where good ideas come from by Steven Johnson* [Video file]. Retrieved from: https://www.youtube.com/watch?v=NugRZGDbPFU

Spira, J.B. (2009. *Intel's War on Information Overload: A Case Study*. Basex. Retrieved from: http://iorgforum.org/wp-content/uploads/2011/06/IntelWarIO.BasexReport1.pdf

State of the American Workplace. (2013). Gallup. Retrieved from http://www.gallup.com/strategicconsulting/163007/state-american-workplace.aspx

Stepper, J. (2014). *The 5 elements of Working Out Loud*. Retrieved from: http://johnstepper.com/2014/01/04/the-5-elements-of-working-out-loud/

Steve Jobs Interview. (1990). Retrieved from: http://openvault.wgbh.org/catalog/7b7ae3-steve-jobs-interview

Surowiecki, J. (2014). *The Cult of Overwork*. The New Yorker. Retrieved from: http://www.newyorker.com/talk/financial/2014/01/27/140127ta_talk_surowiecki

The High Cost of Disengaged Employees. (2002). Gallup Business Journal. Retrieved from: http://businessjournal.gallup.com/content/247/the-high-cost-of-disengaged-employees.aspx

The RSA [The RSA]. (2010, April 1). *RSA Animate - Drive: The surprising truth about what motivates us* [Video file]. Retrieved from: https://www.youtube.com/watch?v=u6XAPnuFjJc

Dan Pink: The puzzle of motivation. (2009). TEDGlobal 2009. Retrieved from: http://www.ted.com/talks/dan_pink_on_motivation

The Shape of Email. (2012). Retrieved from: http://info.mimecast.com/rs/mimecast/images/ShapeofEmailReport-IT.pdf

Townsend, M. & Yeung, S. (2009). *Informal Networks Linked to Success of Change Initiatives.* Retrieved from: http://partneringresources.com/wp-content/uploads/Informal-Networks-Linked-to-Change-Success.pdf

Trotman, A. (2015). *Amazon overtakes Walmart to become largest US retailer.* The Telegraph. Retrieved from: http://www.telegraph.co.uk/finance/newsbysector/retailandconsumer/11759785/Amazon-overtakes-Walmart-to-become-largest-US-retailer.html

Trudell, C., Hagiwara, Y. & Bloomberg, M.J. (2014). *'Gods' Make Comeback at Toyota as Humans Steal Jobs From Robots.* Bloomberg Business. Retrieved from: http://www.bloomberg.com/news/2014-04-06/humans-replacing-robots-herald-toyota-s-vision-of-future.html

Weinberger, D. (2008). *James Boyle.* Joho the blog. Retrieved from: http://www.hyperorg.com/blogger/2008/09/06/ae-james-boyle/

Working Out Loud (2015). Wikipedia, the free encyclopedia. Retrieved from: http://en.wikipedia.org/wiki/Working_Out_Loud

Wright, A. (2008). *Glut: Mastering Information through the Ages.* Cornell University Press.

Wu, L., Lin, C-Y. Aral, S. & Brynjolfsson, E. (2009). *Value of Social Network - A Large-Scale Analysis on Network Structure Impact to Financial Revenue of Information Technology Consultants.* Retrieved from: http://smallblue.research.ibm.com/publications/Utah-ValueOfSocialNetworks.pdf

CPSIA information can be obtained
at www.ICGtesting.com
Printed in the USA
BVHW040256240719
554057BV00065B/1881/P